ST. THOMAS MORE

ALSO BY JOHN F. FINK

Published by ST PAULS

Married Saints

*The Doctors of the Church:
Doctors of the First Millennium*

*The Doctors of the Church:
Doctors of the Second Millennium*

American Saints

Letters to St. Francis de Sales: Mostly on Prayer

Jesus in the Gospels

Biblical Women

By Other Publishers

Moments in Catholic History

Travels With Jesus in the Holy Land

Patriotic Leaders of the Church

Memoirs of a Catholic Journalist

The Mission and Future of the Catholic Press (Editor)

Visit our web site at
www.albahouse.org
(for orders www.stpauls.us)

or call 1-800-343-2522 (ALBA)
and request current catalog

ST. THOMAS
MORE

Model for Modern Catholics

JOHN F. FINK

ST PAULS

Library of Congress Cataloging-in-Publication Data

Fink, John F.
St. Thomas More : model for modern Catholics / by John F. Fink.
    p. cm.
  Includes bibliographical references and index.
  ISBN-13: 978-0-8189-1277-1
  ISBN-10: 0-8189-1277-4
  1. More, Thomas, Sir, Saint, 1478-1535. 2. Henry VIII, King of England,
1491-1547—Relations with humanists. 3. Great Britain—History—Henry VIII,
1509-1547—Biography. 4. Christian martyrs—England—Biography.
5. Statesmen—Great Britain—Biography. 6. Humanists—England—Biography.
7. England—Intellectual life—16th century.   I. Title.
  DA334.M8F56   2008
  942.05'2092—dc22
    [B]   20080031109

Produced and designed in the United States of America by the
Fathers and Brothers of the Society of St. Paul,
2187 Victory Boulevard, Staten Island, New York 10314-6603
as part of their communications apostolate.

ISBN-10: 0-8189-1277-4
ISBN-13: 978-0-8189-1277-1

Printing Information:

Current Printing - first digit   1   2   3   4   5   6   7   8   9   10

Year of Current Printing - first year shown

2009   2010   2011   2012   2013   2014   2015   2016   2017   2018

CONTENTS

FOREWORD

G.K. Chesterton said in 1929, during a visit to Thomas More's home in Chelsea, "Sir Thomas More is more important at this moment than at any moment since his death, even perhaps the great moment of his dying; but he is not quite so important as he will be in a hundred years time. He may come to be counted the greatest Englishman, or, at least, the greatest historical character in English history." I would not limit his importance to *English* history.

Many people know Thomas More mainly because of his dispute with King Henry VIII of England, which resulted in his execution. But Thomas More was much more than that. That's why he was called "A Man for All Seasons" by Robert Bolt in the play by that name. Actually, it was Desiderius Erasmus, More's friend, who first used that phrase to describe More.

Thomas More is a model for modern Catholics, a person that most of us can emulate, especially, perhaps, married men. It's true that he might not have been canonized had he not been martyred but, if not, he should have been. He is possibly the best example of a man who could be eminently successful in secular life while still maintaining the religious practices that can make anyone a saint. As I showed in my chapter about him in my book *Married Saints*, he was also a husband and a father who knew what it was like to live in the bedlam of hectic family life. As we will see, however, there are some things about Thomas that modern husbands would be wise not to copy.

He is known in literary circles as one of the best authors of the Renaissance. He was widely acclaimed as both a poet and an author. A chronology of his published works lists thirty writings, and *The Complete Works of St. Thomas More*, published by Yale University Press, consists of fifteen large volumes. The most famous of his works was *Utopia*, the literary masterpiece he wrote when he was thirty-nine years old. This book opened the door to friendship with other literary figures of his time, although he had been great friends with Erasmus since he first met him when he was only twenty-two. Thomas hosted mainly literary figures and educators at his home; one of the things he was known for was his talents as a host.

He was the most successful lawyer in England and a respected judge. He entered politics and became Speaker of the House of Commons before rising to the highest position, next to the king, in England, viz., Lord Chancellor. By any measure, he was a successful man. Today he is the patron saint of lawyers and politicians.

He was also saintly. As we will see in the following chapters, he was faithful to the daily devotions and penances that he began as a young man. He was a devout Catholic and an ardent defender of the teachings of the Catholic Church against Martin Luther.

Thomas was also known for his wit and sense of humor. He enjoyed jokes. His writings show him to have been a master of satire and humor. Erasmus wrote, "He seems born and made for friendship." He was the type of man we all would like for a friend. His favorite word was "merry"; he used it to such an extent, and he was himself so joyous among his friends, that he was known as "Merry More."

I don't want to give the impression that we should emulate everything about Thomas More. That would be impossible anyway, since he was such a unique guy. But we can certainly learn from his life and that's the purpose of this book.

He was, of course, a martyr and I don't visualize any of us being called to that. That's not the principal way that he's a model although, as I say in the epilogue, Pope Pius XI said at the time of his canonization that he is a model even in his martyrdom because there are "many opportunities for imitating the martyrs without the martyrdom of blood and death." Anyone writing about him must include the circumstances of his death, and this book will do so, but I offer him as a model mainly for the years before his imprisonment and death.

You might have noticed that I have been calling him "Thomas" rather than by his last name. I will continue to do that throughout the book. For one thing, since he is my favorite saint, I have long felt familiar enough with him to do so. And secondly, I hope that you will come to think of him as your friend, one that you could call by his first name. Granted, though, it was not customary in sixteenth century England to call someone by his or her first name, as it is today.

The English language that Thomas used was quite different from today's, as was that of his first biographers. While quoting Thomas and those others who wrote in Middle English, I will put their words in modern English. Some of his modern biographers have not done that, apparently wanting his words to be as authentic as possible, but I prefer to make them as easy for today's reader to understand as possible. Besides, since much of what Thomas wrote was in Latin, those biographers are inconsistent when they translate the Latin but not the Middle English.

I have elected not to use footnotes in this book since I see it as a popular, rather than a scholarly, work. However, my sources are included in the acknowledgments at the end of the book.

I thank Father Edmund C. Lane and his staff at Alba House. There can't be a more thoughtful publisher, or one easier to work with.

ST. THOMAS MORE

CHAPTER 1

HIS FIRST TWENTY-THREE YEARS

Even as a child, an adolescent, and a young man, Thomas More is a model for modern Catholics. His obedience to his father, his studiousness, and his devoutness even as a child are worthy of emulation. However, it is mainly in his struggle to discern his vocation in life that he most serves as a model for us. It's a struggle that we all have. All Catholic men and women should at least consider whether or not God is calling them to the priesthood or religious life, and Thomas did that. As we too should do, Thomas tried to discern how God wanted him to use the gifts he had given to him.

England was in political turmoil during the second half of the fifteenth century. The Hundred Years' War ended in 1453, resulting in the loss to England of all of its previous possessions in France except Calais. At home that war was followed by the Wars of the Roses between 1455 and 1487. The Yorkish King Edward IV was on the throne from 1461 to 1483. Thus he was ruling when Thomas More was born in 1477 or 1478.

Thomas's father, John More, was a lawyer who had somehow become a friend of King Edward IV. Despite the fight for the kingship, London remained a relatively peaceful city and John More was involved in the maintenance and building of the London Bridge. As a lawyer he specialized in city affairs.

1

John More married Agnes Granger on April 24, 1474. It was the first of his four marriages, but it's believed that Agnes was the mother of all six of his children. Thomas was born on either February 6 or 7, and there's dispute over whether it was in 1477 or 1478; the latter seems the more likely and we will assume that it is correct. He was named after Saint Thomas Becket, who by coincidence had been born three hundred sixty years earlier only twenty yards from the More home on Milk Street. Thomas was a popular name in England. Indeed, five other Thomases were to play significant roles in Thomas More's life: Thomas Wolsey, Thomas Cromwell, Thomas Howard, Thomas Cranmer, and Thomas Audley.

Both Thomas More's older and younger sisters, Joan and Elizabeth, married lawyers and a younger brother, John, acted as a secretary to Thomas later in life but died in his thirties. The other two children, Agatha and Edward, apparently died as children, perhaps in an epidemic of the "sweating sickness" that invaded London in 1485.

His Father's Influence

Thomas's mother died when he was a child but again, we're not sure when—possibly also in 1485. Neither she nor the stepmothers Thomas had from his father's three additional marriages seem to have had an influence on him. His father, though, very definitely did. John More attended very closely to Thomas's personal and professional development. The relationship between John and Thomas More has received considerable attention. There's dispute over exactly how much of Thomas's life was dictated by his father. We know that, as in most English households at the end of the fifteenth century, there was strict discipline in the More home. Thomas obeyed his father, there's no doubt about that, and John certainly wanted Thomas to follow him in the legal profession, but that doesn't necessarily mean that John insisted that Thomas become a lawyer.

Thomas deeply respected his father. Thomas's biographers describe a scene when he was Lord Chancellor of England. He would go to Westminster Hall to preside over the Court of Chancery. John More at the time was a justice of the King's Bench that met in the same hall. Whenever Thomas would pass his father, he knelt down before him and asked for his blessing, just as he had been accustomed to do every morning and evening when he was a child.

Thomas's love for his father, and his acknowledgment of what he owed to him, was expressed in the epitaph that Thomas wrote for himself. It's surprising that so much of it is devoted to his father. What follows is the beginning of the epitaph Thomas wrote for himself, not for his father:

> At last John More his father, Knight and chosen by the prince to be one of the justices of the King's bench, a civil man, pleasant, harmless, gentle, pitiful, just and uncorrupted, in years old but in body more than for his years lusty, after he had perceived his life so long lengthened that he saw his son Lord Chancellor of England, thinking himself now to have lived long enough, gladly departed to God. His son then, his father being dead, to whom as long as he lived, being compared, was wont both to be called young and himself so thought too, missing his father departed and seeing four children of his own and of their offspring eleven, began in his own conceit to wax old.

Thomas's Education

When Thomas was seven, his father enrolled him in Saint Anthony's Grammar School, which had a demanding curriculum. Lessons began at six in the morning and continued until six in the evening. There were prayers in the morning and evening.

The students learned to converse in Latin, a skill that would serve Thomas well in later life. For example, he could communicate with his friend Erasmus only in Latin since Erasmus couldn't speak English. Thomas's prayer books were in Latin and most of the books and letters he wrote were in Latin. Grammar and rhetoric were the primary courses at Saint Anthony's and Thomas proved himself a brilliant student. His five years there served him well.

Usually the boys at Saint Anthony's moved on to Eton, but Thomas had a greater opportunity. While Thomas was in grammar school, King Edward IV died in 1483. His son Edward V was probably murdered in the Tower of London by his uncle, who became King Richard III. Richard was killed in the Battle of Bosworth Field in 1485, and Henry Tudor claimed the throne as King Henry VII. Through all this, though, Archbishop John Morton served as Archbishop of Canterbury and Lord Chancellor of England.

When Thomas was twelve, John More managed to secure for him a two-year period of service as a page at Lambeth Palace, where Archbishop Morton and England's other leading ecclesiastical and civic officials worked. His duties included serving the archbishop and his guests at table, but there was also a private school for the boys in the household. Thomas apparently caught the eye of the archbishop. In his biography of his father-in-law, William Roper wrote that Archbishop Morton once told his dinner guests, "This child here waiting at the table, whosoever shall live to see it, will prove a marvelous man." It's not impossible to think that Archbishop Morton actually envisioned Thomas as achieving the position he then held as both Archbishop of Canterbury and Lord Chancellor of England.

That Thomas was just as impressed with Archbishop Morton is clear from his treatment of the man in his later books *Utopia* and *The History of Richard III*. In the latter work, he described the archbishop as "a man of great natural wit, very well learned, and honorable in behavior, lacking no wise ways to win favor." He was particularly impressed with the way the archbishop had been able to bring an end to the Wars of the Roses, arranging the marriage between Henry VII and Elizabeth of York.

After Thomas spent two years as a page at Lambeth Palace, Archbishop Morton sponsored Thomas as a scholarship student at Oxford University. He was then all of fourteen years old. Oxford in those days was quite different from the Oxford University of today. It had about a thousand students scattered among its various colleges, many of them studying for the priesthood. It seems probable that Archbishop Morton hoped that Thomas, too, would discern a vocation to the priesthood—which, however, would not have pleased John More. Thomas was in Canterbury College, which was run by Benedictine monks, and Archbishop Morton undoubtedly thought that it was a good preparation for a successful ecclesiastical career.

Besides being enrolled in Canterbury College, Thomas apparently was also a member of Saint Mary's Hall in Oxford. This might be compared with a residence hall or even a fraternity in today's American colleges because the students lived in the halls as a family or household. In the case of Saint Mary's Hall, the twenty or so students would rise at five o'clock in the morning for Mass before attending a morning lecture at six. After a light breakfast, there was usually a second lecture at nine o'clock. Dinner was at ten or eleven and supper at five. Bedtime was normally at eight or nine.

Just as at Saint Anthony's, the students were expected to converse only in Latin. The morning lectures, also in Latin, included disputations, so the students quickly learned public debate. Much as debates in our modern colleges, the students were expected to argue either side of a proposition. Already at age sixteen, Thomas showed signs of becoming a great orator. It was also during his days at Oxford that he began to write poetry—highly accomplished poetry.

Thomas remained at Oxford, though, for only two years.

Many of his biographers have written that John More insisted that he return to London and prepare for a life as a lawyer. Erasmus, in fact, wrote that John threatened to disinherit his son if he didn't embark on a legal career. It's believed that, left to his own preferences, Thomas would not have become a lawyer since his preferences in school were for theology and the other liberal arts—literature, history, and philosophy. One of his biographers, though, Peter Ackroyd, doubts that Thomas had to be persuaded to become a lawyer. He had been schooled in the arts of persuasion, as a debater and orator and as a rhetorician, and it seemed that these skills were well suited to a life as a lawyer. Ackroyd wrote, "The role of lawyer suited his temperament. He was a resourceful actor and he became an equally skillful rhetorician; in later life he was sought by both Court and City for his gifts as an orator."

At any rate, whether at his father's insistence or because of his own willingness, Thomas left Oxford at age sixteen and entered New Inn, one of at least ten Inns of Chancery in London where young men prepared for the legal profession. These inns probably developed from the hostels where lawyers stayed while they worked at the nearby courts. At the end of the fifteenth century, each inn had about a hundred students who were trained in aspects of English common law.

He was a member of New Inn for two years before moving on to Lincoln's Inn for advanced legal training. John More was a respected senior member of Lincoln's Inn while his son was there. Thomas studied law there for five years before he was called to the bar at age twenty-three.

Life in a Carthusian Monastery

Although he studied at Lincoln's Inn for five years, for part of the time he didn't live there. Like so many young men in their late teens and early twenties, then and now, Thomas was trying to discern his vocation in life. To what was God calling him? As William Roper wrote about his father-in-law, "He gave himself to devotion and prayer in the Charterhouse of London, religiously living there, without vow, about four years."

It's not clear, however, that he was actually "living there," because Cresacre More, another biographer, wrote that his great-grandfather lived "near the Charterhouse, frequenting daily their spiritual exercises without any vow." Both are possibilities. The Charterhouse had accommodations for guests who could lodge there for a period of time (for a fee, of course), but it was also possible to find temporary lodgings nearby. It seems more likely, though, that Thomas would have preferred to live in the Charterhouse, as Roper wrote, and traveled from there to Lincoln's Inn during the day.

Thomas's biographers, including Roper, are not sure which four years of his life he spent at the Charterhouse. Some date them as late as from 1501 to 1505, which would have been after he completed his study at Lincoln's Inn and was beginning to practice the legal profession.

The Charterhouse was a Carthusian monastery, more formally called the Carthusian House of the Salutation of the Blessed Virgin Mary, established in the 1370s from a gift from Sir Walter de Mauny. The Carthusian Order, founded by Saint Bruno in 1084, is considered the strictest of the Catholic religious orders. It has been said of the Carthusian Order that it has never been reformed since it was never corrupted. The men spent most of their time in individual cells, although they were called to pray together at all hours of the day and night, beginning shortly after midnight. They had a sparse diet, with no meat. During the day, in solitude, they worked in their cells.

The Charterhouse remains today to the north of Smithfield in London, but in Thomas's day it was beyond the western gates of London. Still, it was not more than a five-minute ride from Lincoln's Inn. It had a special entrance for guests and a staircase leading to guest cells on the upper floor so they would not disturb the monks. Unlike the monks, who ate in their cells, there was a dining room for guests. With these accommodations available, why would Thomas live only *near* the Charterhouse?

Guests were permitted to view the monks from a stone gallery above the chapel, and Thomas More did so regularly. Since he lived there (or near there) for four years, it's possible that he was also permitted to participate in the monks' life of prayer. Certainly he learned their ways of austere living because it was during this time that he worked at developing his prayer life and achieving self-mastery. He began some of the spiritual practices that he would maintain the rest of his life. He attended Mass daily, prayed and fasted regularly, limited the number of hours he slept, and began to wear a hair shirt—a shirt with hair that rubbed against the skin. For the rest of his life, his hours didn't exactly correspond to those of the Carthusians, but they differed from his contemporaries. He rose in the morning at two o'clock and began each day with prayer, including the Divine Office, followed by religious studies and attendance at Mass. (Admittedly, most people in the sixteenth century, before electric lights, rose and retired earlier than we do today; Thomas's two o'clock would probably correspond to our four o'clock.)

Thomas also had access at the Charterhouse to religious books. Printing from movable type had been invented by Johann Gutenberg earlier in the fifteenth century (his forty-two line Bible was printed in 1455), so books were relatively rare items. One of the principal occupations of the monks at the Charterhouse was still the copying of manuscripts. But its library did have some books, two of which were an influence on Thomas— *Scale of Perfection*, by Walter Hilton, and *The Imitation of Christ*, by Thomas à Kempis—both of which he mentioned in his writings as books to "nourish and increase devotion."

The *Imitation*, perhaps actually written by Gerhard Groote and edited by Thomas à Kempis, has been ranked second only to the Bible in its impact on the worldwide Christian community. Other possible authors mentioned at one time or another include Saint Bernard of Clairvaux, Pope Innocent III, and Jean Gerson of the University of Paris. (Thomas More thought that Gerson wrote it.) The emphasis throughout the book is that living the Christian life consists, not in what we know or believe, but in who we are and how we imitate Christ in his sufferings. It encouraged each reader to find his or her (of course, it said only "his") cross and bear it willingly. It's possible that Thomas decided to start wearing his hair shirt after reading *The Imitation of Christ*. *Introduction to the Devout Life*, by Saint Francis de Sales, wouldn't be written for more than a hundred years after Thomas read *The Imitation of Christ* or he surely would have studied it. One difference between the two books is that the *Imitation* was originally written for monks while the *Introduction* was written for lay men and women.

The other book that influenced Thomas was *Scale of Perfection*, by Walter Hilton. While the *Imitation* was written for monks, Hilton's book described the rewards of a vocation as an active Christian layman in the secular world. It urged its readers to "know the gifts which are given us of God" and contrasted the apostles John and Peter, John being a contemplative while Peter was an activist. Perhaps this book eventually influenced Thomas more than the *Imitation*.

DISCERNING HIS VOCATION

We don't know if Thomas seriously considered becoming a Carthusian monk. If so, he didn't mention it to any of his contemporaries except, perhaps, to his daughter Meg shortly before his death. He did, though, consider becoming a priest. He discussed this possibility with William Lily, first high master of Saint Paul's School. Erasmus, too, wrote that Thomas thought about becoming a priest, as we'll see when we consider his decision to marry.

Undoubtedly, though, the one who knew most about the

struggle Thomas was having with his vocation was John Colet, his spiritual advisor. Colet was a classical scholar, theologian, humanist, and one of the leaders of the Renaissance in England. Like some of his contemporaries, he made the long pilgrimage from England to Italy. He lectured on the New Testament at Oxford from 1496 to 1504, but this was after Thomas left Oxford in 1494. From 1504 to 1519 he was dean of Saint Paul's Cathedral and he endowed and founded Saint Paul's School in 1509. It's not clear exactly when he and Thomas became close friends but he exerted a profound effect on Thomas.

During this period, when Thomas was twenty or twenty-one, he wasn't only discerning whether or not to become a priest, he also questioned whether he should be a lawyer. His interests lay with the liberal arts—literature, history, philosophy and theology. Even while studying law and praying with the Carthusians at the Charterhouse, he somehow found time to immerse himself in those studies. He developed his writing style and composed epigrams, usually in Latin, as a hobby. He soon became associated with other scholars who later became known as the "More circle," but Thomas was the youngest of the group.

We have already met John Colet and, briefly, William Lily, master of Saint Paul's School. The others were William Grocyn and Thomas Linacre. All of them except Colet had studied at Oxford University (Colet went to Cambridge) and then had made the journey to Italy. Linacre had studied at the Court of Lorenzo the Magnificent in Florence as well as in Padua and Rome. He received a degree in medicine at Padua and when he returned to London he practiced medicine while teaching Greek. Thomas was one of his students in Greek. Grocyn, a priest, also taught Greek, at Oxford, after his return from Italy. He then received the "benefice" of Saint Lawrence Jewry Church, located near John More's home on Milk Street. Thomas learned Greek from him.

FRIENDSHIP WITH DESIDERIUS ERASMUS

Finally, there was Desiderius Erasmus. He was born illegitimately in Gouda, a suburb of the Dutch city of Rotterdam, in 1466—so he was twelve years older than Thomas. He was orphaned at thirteen when his parents died of the plague. He was sent by his guardians to the Augustinian monastery of Saint Gregory where a relaxed discipline allowed him to read pagan classics as well as the Scriptures and the Church Fathers. He was ordained a priest in 1492. Three years later he studied in Paris. He quickly earned a reputation for eloquence and learning. To earn a living in Paris, he taught rhetoric and for a while was resident tutor in a home for the sons of English nobles. It was there that he met William Blount, Lord Mountjoy, who urged him to visit England.

Erasmus arrived in England during the summer of 1499, when Thomas was twenty-one, still studying law at Lincoln's Inn and living at the Charterhouse. Erasmus stayed at the country house of Lord Mountjoy in Greenwich. One day Thomas and a friend from Lincoln's Inn, Edward Arnold, arrived. Sometime during the day, Thomas suggested that they all walk to the village of Eltham to visit the royal palace there. Prince Henry, who was nine years old at the time, was there, and both Thomas and Arnold presented him with some writings for the occasion. When Erasmus wrote about this incident some twenty-four years later, he said that he was annoyed at the time at not having been warned about the visit to the palace so he could have prepared some of his own verses.

This incident is intriguing because it tells us something about Thomas's social status at the time, that he was allowed access to England's royal family apparently without an appointment, and that he was permitted to bring a companion. It was apparently the first time he met Prince Henry, who later would play such an important role in his life—and death.

Erasmus remained in England until January 1500, when

he returned to France. By that time a great friendship had developed between him and Thomas. Erasmus also met Thomas's friends Grocyn and Colet and was particularly impressed with Colet. Thomas and Erasmus began corresponding with each other and much of what we know about Thomas comes from this correspondence. They encouraged one another in their writings and promoted each other's publications. For example, Erasmus set to work on his first book, *Adagiorum Collectanea*, shortly after he returned to France. It was published just six months after he left England and Thomas actively encouraged its publication.

INFLUENCE OF SAINT AUGUSTINE

Meanwhile, during his studies of the Church Fathers, Thomas became a disciple of Saint Augustine. Colet might have been the one who introduced him to this great theologian because he had a particular dislike for the theology of Saint Thomas Aquinas, especially his *Summa Theologica*, and preferred Augustine. He wrote that he liked the emphasis on love rather than knowledge: "It is beyond doubt more pleasing to God himself to be loved by men than to be surveyed, and to be worshiped than to be understood." (In this there's a similarity with Pope Benedict XVI, who also preferred Augustine's theology to that of Aquinas.) Thomas studied the writings of Saint Augustine while he was living in the Charterhouse, probably at Colet's urging.

Sometime during that period of his life, in his early twenties and before he was called to the bar, Grocyn asked Thomas to give a series of lectures in Saint Lawrence Jewry on *The City of God*, the thousand-page book that Augustine wrote during the last two decades of his life. (At the same time, Colet asked Grocyn to lecture at Saint Paul's Cathedral on the pseudo-Dionysius.) Thomas's lectures attracted an unusually large congregation. Unfortunately, none of the lectures have survived, although biographer Thomas Stapleton noted that he approached the book "not from the theological point of view, but from the standpoint of history and philosophy." However, just the fact that he was able to attract a large crowd at his young age indicates that he already had a reputation as an intellectual and good speaker.

Augustine's book saw the history of the world as two cities, the city of God and the city of the world, the one existing within the other. We can imagine Thomas wondering if he could live in the city of God while remaining active in the city of the world.

Translation of *Life of Pico della Mirandola*

While Thomas was still living in the Charterhouse and trying to discern his vocation, Colet gave him another book, the biography of Pico della Mirandola, a young Italian scholar and philosopher who died in 1494 at the young age of thirty-one. Colet had become familiar with Pico's works while he was in Italy and had annotated his commentary on Genesis. Thomas was obviously fascinated with Pico. He translated the life of Pico into English and perhaps used it as a sort of spiritual handbook. The immediate reason for the translation, though, was to present it as a present to a friend, Joyce Leigh, who had been admitted to the order of the Poor Clares. Some years later Thomas's brother-in-law, John Rastell, published the translation. It was the first of Thomas's published works.

Pico was a layman who, Thomas believed, should have been a monk. At the end of the book, in fact, Pico is burning in purgatory because he had a vocation to be a friar but didn't accept the call. (He was, though, buried in the habit of a Dominican.) Thomas wrote that Pico possessed "an incredible wit" and "a marvelous fast memory," that "he was of cheer always merry and of so benign nature he was never troubled with anger" and always displayed "a pleasant and a merry countenance." These later became descriptions of Thomas himself.

Pico also "gave himself day and night most fervently to the study of Scripture," prayed at set hours of the day, gave alms freely to the poor, practiced austere mortifications, and devoted his life to the defense of the Church. Nevertheless, he ended up in purgatory because he was negligent in his duties, ungrateful for the gifts he received, and was slow in following God's will.

Thomas appended prayers and poems to his translation. He turned some of Pico's spiritual precepts into powerful poetry, meant to "stir thee to prayer," a prayer of contemplation that "not only presents the mind to the Father, but also unites it with him by unspeakable ways which only they know who have tried it."

The following passage gives us a good insight into Thomas's own prayer life at this stage of his life:

> I care not how long or how short your prayer is, but how effectual, how ardent, how interrupted and broken with sighs rather than drawn out at length with an endless number of words. If you love your health; if you desire to be secure from the snares of the devil, from the storms of this world, from the hands of your enemies; if you long to be acceptable to God; if you covet everlasting happiness—then let no day pass without at least once presenting yourself to God in prayer, falling down before him flat on the ground with a humble affection and a devout mind; not merely with your lips, but from the innermost recesses of your heart, crying out these words of the prophet: "The sins of my youth and my frailties remember not, but in your mercy remember me because of your goodness, O Lord" (Psalm 25:7).

A unique part of the book is entitled "The Twelve Properties of a Lover." It's a long thirteen-part love ballad, each part
with two sections. The first describes some aspect of human
love while the second applies that to the love of God. This is
followed by two more poems, "The Twelve Rules of Spiritual
Battle" and "The Twelve Weapons of Spiritual Battle." Finally,
the book ends with a lengthy prayer that emphasizes the goodness and generosity of God. The finished product was a masterpiece of spirituality and poetry, especially for a man in his
early twenties.

Thomas was called to the bar, became a lawyer in 1501
at age twenty-three. In 1502 an event occurred that would
significantly affect Thomas's life, although there was no way
anyone could have known that at the time. Prince Arthur died.
He was the eldest son of King Henry VII and his death made
Prince Henry the heir. Prince Arthur had married Catherine of
Aragon in 1501 and that marriage, too, was to figure in Thomas's
future.

CHAPTER 2

HUSBAND AND FATHER

Although the courtship of both of his wives leaves much to be desired by our standards, Thomas was a faithful husband and an excellent father. Unfortunately, not many men take as active a role in the secular education and religious training of their children as Thomas did. Perhaps most modern parents will consider it impractical to completely emulate Thomas in today's society, but surely his example should encourage parents to fulfill their responsibilities in the rearing of their children.

In struggling with his vocation, Thomas finally discerned that his calling was definitely to married life. According to Erasmus, Thomas decided that his calling was to become "a chaste husband rather than a licentious priest." Thomas himself wrote that, during his adolescence, his struggle with his sexuality brought him almost to the "very gates of hell." In one of his writings when he was forty-one, he wrote about his father's parental wisdom when Thomas, then sixteen, had become infatuated with a fourteen-year-old girl. "On his account," Thomas wrote, "a chaperon was imposed upon us, and a door strong enough to thwart our very destiny kept apart a pair whom the stars wished to bring together."

There is no reason to believe, though, that Thomas was any more hot blooded or more quickly sexually aroused than any other young man. Even that remark by Erasmus sounds like something Thomas probably said to him in jest; he often joked like that. Nevertheless, it seems true that Thomas made his decision at least partly because he didn't want to take, or felt unable to take, a vow of celibacy.

The one who knew most about Thomas's spiritual life was John Colet, his confessor and spiritual advisor. At one time, while Colet was away, Thomas wrote to him, expressing his dependence upon Colet's advice:

> It has been my custom to rely on your prudent advice, to find my recreation in your pleasant company, to be stirred by your powerful sermons, to be edified by your life and example, to be guided, in fine, by even the slightest indications of your opinions. When I had the advantage of all these helps, I used to feel strengthened, now that I am deprived of them, I seem to languish and grow feeble. By following your footsteps I had escaped from almost the very gates of hell and now, driven by some secret but irresistible force, I am falling back again into the gruesome darkness.

We're not sure what he meant by that last sentence, but it's believed that Colet advised Thomas to answer his vocation to married life.

How to Choose a Wife

Having made his decision, Thomas set out to find a wife. He doesn't seem to have been the most romantic man, but he was practical—if, perhaps, a bit naïve or idealistic. He even wrote a poem that he called "How to Choose a Wife" in which he wrote, "True love is inspired, with happy promise, by respect for a woman's glorious virtue—a noble gift which endures, does not fail in sickness, does not perish with the years."

In searching for a wife, Thomas advised that a man must "observe what kind of parents the lady has.… See to it that her mother is revered for the excellence of her character, which is sucked in and expressed by her tender and impressionable little girl."

But there was more:

Next, see to this: what sort of personality she has; how agreeable she is. Let her maidenly countenance be calm and without severity. But let her modesty bring blushes to her cheeks; let her glance not be provocative. Let her be mild-mannered, not throwing her slender arms wantonly around men's necks. Let her glances be restrained; let her have no roving eye. Let her pretty lips always be free of pointless garrulity and also of boorish taciturnity.

He wanted a wife who would be a lifetime companion, who could engage him with "pleasant and intelligent conversation" while helping him to raise their children according to "right principles."

With this girl of his dreams in mind, Thomas began his serious search. He thought he found her in the household of Sir John Colt, a titled landowner in Essex, about fifteen miles from London. The Colt and More families knew one another well and it appears that Thomas had frequently been at Netherhall, the Colts' country estate, with a red-brick mansion and even complete with a moat and drawbridge. Jane Colt, the eldest daughter, was only sixteen, ten years younger than Thomas, and we know nothing about their courtship. From all accounts, both were inexperienced when it came to romance and Thomas's biographers insist that he was shy around women.

We do have a statement from William Roper, Thomas's son-in-law and first biographer, that Thomas was first attracted to a younger daughter but thought that "it would be both grief and shame to the eldest to see her younger sister in marriage preferred before her." Therefore, he married Jane. Even if Roper got this story directly from Thomas, it appears doubtful. Jane was only sixteen and a younger sister would certainly not have been of marriageable age. It's already amazing that Thomas chose a sixteen-year-old who would have been hard-pressed to engage him with "pleasant and intelligent conversation" since she had not had nearly the education that Thomas had had.

Marriage Was Hard for Jane

Thomas and Jane were married in January 1505, a month before his twenty-seventh birthday. Married life must have been difficult for Jane, who had spent all her life in the country with seventeen brothers and sisters. Now she was living with a man ten years older, a scholar and lawyer, who always wore a hair shirt and who began his day at two o'clock in the morning.

Apparently there were problems in the marriage at first, if Erasmus is a reliable reporter. In his book *Colloquies*, he wrote about a couple who certainly were Thomas and Jane. The story is worth quoting at length:

> I am intimate with a gentleman of good family, learned and of particularly keen wit. He married a young woman, a maiden of seventeen, who had been brought up entirely in the country at her father's house, as men in his position prefer to live in the country most of the time for the sake of hunting and fowling. My friend wished to have a simple, unaffected maid so that he might the more easily train her in his own tastes. He began by instructing her in literature and music and to accustom her by degrees to repeat the discourses she heard and to teach her other things that would afterwards be of use to her.

Now all this was completely new to the girl who had been brought up at home to do nothing but chatter and amuse herself; she soon grew weary of this life and would no longer submit to her husband's wishes. When he expostulated with her, she would weep, day after day, and, sometimes, throw herself flat on the ground, beating her head as if she wished for death.

As there seemed to be no way of ending this, he concealed his annoyance and invited his wife to spend a holiday with him in his father-in-law's house in the country; to this she most willingly agreed. When they got there, the husband left his wife with her mother and sisters and went hunting with his father-in-law; he took the opportunity of taking him apart from any witnesses and of telling him that whereas he had hoped his daughter would prove an agreeable companion for life, he now had one who was always weeping and moaning, nor could she be cured by scolding; he begged his father-in-law to help him in curing this distemper.

The father-in-law replied that he gave him his daughter once for all; that if she refused to obey his commands, he should exercise his rights and correct her by blows. "I know my rights," said the son-in-law, "but rather than resort to this desperate remedy I'd prefer to have her cured by your skill or authority." The father-in-law promised to attend to the matter.

A day or so later he seized an opportunity to be alone with his daughter. Then, putting on a stern look, he began to recall how homely she was, how ill-mannered, how often he had feared he would be unable to find her a husband. "But," he said, "with the greatest difficulty I found you a husband such as any girl, however favored, would long for. And yet, not recognizing what I've done for you, or realizing that you have such a husband—who would scarcely think you fit for one of his maidservants if he weren't the kindest of men—you rebel against him."

To make a long story short, the father's speech grew so heated that he seemed barely able to keep his hands off her. Moved partly by fear, partly by the truth, the girl promptly went down on her knees before her father, begging forgiveness for the past and swearing she would be mindful of her duty in the future. He pardoned her, promising to be a most affectionate father if she carried out her promise.

The girl went to her bedroom, met her husband privately, fell on her knees before him, and said, "Husband, up to this time I have known neither you nor myself. Hereafter you shall see me a changed person; only forget the past." Her husband received this speech with a kiss and promised her everything if she kept her word. Thereafter, there was nothing, however lowly, that she did not do promptly and willingly when her husband wished, so strong was the love born and confirmed between them.

Obviously, we in the twenty-first century can hardly condone everything in that story. It shows the lowly role of women in sixteenth-century England. Further, it seems wrong for Thomas to have confided in Erasmus so much, if the story actually happened. As it stands, though, the story certainly sounds plausible and it's true that Thomas and Jane settled down to a happy life. She studied Latin and learned how to play the viol, the spinet and the flute. She was a gracious hostess to the many guests (including Erasmus) Thomas invited into their home.

Jane also bore Thomas's children. They came quickly—four children in five-and-a-half years—three girls and a boy. Margaret (called Meg) was born in 1505, Elizabeth in 1506, Cecily in 1507, and John in 1509.

The Family Home for Twenty Years

They were living in a house in Bucklersbury that Thomas had leased from the Mercers prior to their marriage. The Mercers were one of the sixty or so guilds or fraternities of merchants in London for whom Thomas did legal work. The house was known as the Old Barge because the street in front of the house had been the Walbrook that flowed to the Thames River and boats came up the Walbrook and moored outside the Barge. The brook had since been paved over.

The Old Barge was a large and roomy stone building with elaborate gardens behind it. At first Thomas leased only part of the house, but leased all of it eight years later.

It included bedrooms and parlors, a chapel, studies, great hall and courtyard, the gallery, servants' quarters and stables for their horses. It was located in a noisy neighborhood, with merchants of all kinds selling their wares. Here is where Thomas was to spend most of his adult life, twenty years, until he and his family moved to Chelsea in 1525.

Directly across the street from the Barge was Saint Stephen Walbrook, a church of ancient foundation but rebuilt about a hundred years before Thomas and Jane moved into the neighborhood. This is where Thomas attended daily Mass, served at the altar, sang in the choir (apparently not very well), and participated in processions. (Of course, this was before lay men and women could be lectors or extraordinary ministers of Holy Communion.) It was filled with pictures and statues. It was a typical, but wealthy, London church.

Erasmus visited the Old Barge for the first time in the spring of 1505, shortly after Jane and Thomas's wedding, and this undoubtedly was the first time Jane and Erasmus had met each other. Probably, too, this was when Thomas confided in Erasmus his early marital problems. We don't know what Jane thought about the Dutchman, who was not an easy man to please. He spoke no English and was always fussy.

Erasmus returned to England in 1509 and again stayed with the Mores. By this time there were four children under five, and we have to wonder how Jane was able to cope with him. He wrote about his visit, "I was staying with More after my return from Italy when I was kept several days in the house with lumbago. My library had not arrived; and if it had, my illness forbade exertion in more serious studies." Therefore, he said, he wrote the work for which he is most noted: *Encomium Moriae* or *Praise of Folly*. We'll say more about that book later, but the point here is that Jane More probably had to supervise the nursing of Erasmus while caring for her children, at the same time playing hostess for Erasmus's friends who undoubtedly visited him and Thomas during those three months.

By 1511, when Thomas was thirty-three, his law practice was growing quickly and he was beginning to make a name for himself with his writings. He had a happy marriage and four small children. Life was very good for Thomas More.

That year Erasmus was in Paris when he remembered that he had left some books in his study in the Mores' home at Bucklersbury. Rather than writing to Thomas about the matter, he wrote to Andrew Ammonius, an Italian scholar who at the time was enjoying the Mores' hospitality. When sending the books to him on May 19, 1511, Ammonius included a letter in which he said, "Our dear and beloved More and his kind wife who never thinks of you without a blessing upon you, are well, together with their children and the whole household."

Then, only three months later, tragedy struck. Jane More, only twenty-two, became ill and died, quite unexpectedly. Perhaps it was the sweating sickness, or influenza, or any of the other illnesses that afflicted London. Perhaps, too, she died in childbirth along with the child; Erasmus suggested that. If so, Thomas never mentioned it. She was buried in Saint Stephen Walbrook. Twenty years later Thomas moved her body to Chelsea to lie in the grave he planned for himself.

Apart from his grief, Thomas had the pressing difficulty of caring for four young children. The priest at Saint Stephen Walbrook, Father John Bouge, reports what happened next: "Within a month, he came to me on a Sunday late at night and there he brought me a dispensation to be married the next Monday without asking any banns." Against the advice of his friends and common custom, Thomas remarried within thirty days of Jane's death.

Within his wide circle of friends he knew many women who were not married, some older and some younger. He chose Alice Middleton, a woman seven years older than he. He was thirty-three, she forty. Both had been widowed. Alice's first husband, John Middleton, had been a wealthy silk merchant. He and Thomas were both members of the Mercers' Company. Alice's family owned a manor and estates in Essex, near the Colts. So it's probable that Thomas and Alice had known each other for some time, probably even before Thomas met Jane. Alice was married to John Middleton the first time Thomas was looking for a wife.

With his second marriage, Thomas gained a stepchild. Alice's daughter, also named Alice, came to live at Bucklersbury.

Needless to say, Alice was considerably different from Jane. For one thing, she was eighteen years older and as set in her habits as most forty-year-olds. She proved to be a loving stepmother to Thomas's four children, making sure that they carried out the duties and studies Thomas assigned to them. She even tried to learn a little Latin as well as how to play the lute, lyre and recorder. Thomas, too, learned to play the lute enough that they could play duets.

Alice ran the household, and she was not as willing as Jane had been to put up with long-staying guests. Ammonius got the hint after a long stay and moved out. He wrote to Erasmus that it was a relief to get away "from the hooked beak of the harpy." Some years later Erasmus also moved out of the Barge and wrote in a letter, "I feel myself becoming a stale guest to More's wife." Nevertheless, even Erasmus grew to like Alice. He wrote about her:

> More did not however long remain single but, contrary to his friends' advice, he married a widow, more for the sake of the management of his household than to please his own fancy, as she is no great beauty nor yet young, "*nec bella admodum nec puella*" (neither a girl or a pearl) as he sometimes laughingly says, but a sharp and watchful housewife; with whom, nevertheless, he lives on as sweet and pleasant terms as if she were as young and lovely as anyone could desire; and scarcely any husband obtains from his wife by masterfulness and severity as much compliance as he does by blandishments and jests.

Dame Alice could hold her own when it came to jests. In one letter from Thomas to Erasmus, he ended, "My wife desires to send a million compliments, especially for your careful wish that she may live for many years. She says she is the more anxious for this as she will then live the longer to plague me." Of course, that might have been Thomas's humor rather than something Alice actually said.

Several of Thomas's biographers repeated the tale that one day, after she had confessed her sins at church, she said to Thomas, "You can be merry for I have finished with my past nagging and now intend to start afresh."

Actually, it appears that Thomas needed some nagging, especially when it came to his appearance. He was notoriously indifferent toward what he wore. Erasmus noted that his clothes were often crooked, crumpled, even dirty. By contrast, Alice was meticulous about her dress.

As Thomas became ever more involved in his law practice and his public service, including long absences from London, Alice became more responsible for maintaining the household and caring for the children. There can be no doubt that Thomas trusted her judgment completely.

Thomas composed the following tribute to both of his wives above the grave that he expected to be his, Jane's and Alice's:

> Within his tomb Jane, wife of More reclines;
> This for himself and Alice More designs.
> The first—dear object of my youthful vow,
> Gave me three daughters and a son to know.
> The next—ah virtue in a step-dame rare,
> Nursed my sweet infants with a mother's care.
> With both my years so happily have passed,
> Which the more dear, I know not—first of last
> O! had religion: destiny allowed,
> How smoothly, mixed, had our three fortunes flowed.
> But be we in the tomb—in heaven allied;
> So kinder death shall grant what life denied.

THOMAS'S HOME BECOMES A SCHOOL

The More household consisted mainly of females. Besides Alice and her daughter Alice, there were Thomas's three daughters, Margaret Giggs, Anne Cresacre, and Frances Staverton. Margaret Giggs was an adopted daughter, possibly a distant cousin; when Thomas wrote to his children he addressed letters, "Thomas More to his dearest children and to Margaret Giggs whom he numbers among his own" or "Thomas More to Margaret, Elizabeth, Cecily, his dear daughters, and to Margaret Giggs as dear as though she was his daughter." Anne Cresacre was Thomas's ward. An orphan, she had inherited estates as well as some income. As her guardian, Thomas was responsible for her estates until she came of age. (When she did, she married Thomas's only son, John.) Frances Staverton was a niece who also lived at Bucklersbury for a time.

So Thomas was directly responsible for the education of seven girls and one son. Perhaps because of that, he became the first Englishman seriously to consider the education of women at the same level as that of men. His home became a school. Not only were his children home schooled, but in later years there were between eleven and thirteen wards or grandchildren being educated there, too. Thomas was careful when hiring tutors to ensure that they were interested in teaching girls as well as boys. Margaret (Meg) eventually became the most learned woman of her day, at least in England. Margaret Giggs, the adopted daughter, became one of the first women in England to study medicine. She married John Clements, the family's first tutor who went on to become a doctor, and helped him in his work.

The school at Bucklersbury began when Meg was six years old, shortly after Thomas's second wedding, and, of course, the curriculum expanded as the years went on. Eventually the children would learn Latin and Greek as well as logic, geometry, astronomy, science, history, literature, philosophy, and music. They were taught to listen carefully enough to sermons they heard that they could deliver them, both in Latin and English. When Thomas was traveling out of the country, he would write to his daughters in Latin. One of them would translate it into English and then another would translate the English back into Latin. In addition, each child was expected to write a letter to Thomas, in Latin, every day. Despite his busy schedule, he answered each one.

Naturally, the letters became more learned as the children aged. Thomas once sent some essays the children had written in Latin to Erasmus for his comments. He replied that he was amazed by their style and subject matter. He had once taken no interest in the education of girls but Thomas's daughters changed his mind.

The education he planned and supervised for his children was, in fact, so successful that the school in his home became famous throughout Europe. Some of his closest friends were the most noted educators of Christendom, classical scholars who wrote a great deal about education.

In a letter to William Gonell, one of his children's tutors, Thomas explained his philosophy of education. Regardless of the subject, he wrote, Gonell should

> esteem most whatever may teach them piety towards God, charity to all, and modesty and Christian humility in themselves. The whole fruit of their endeavors should consist in the testimony of God and good conscience. Thus they will be inwardly calm and at peace and neither stirred by praise of flatterers nor stung by the follies of unlearned mockers of learning.

DISCIPLINE IN THE MORE HOME

The More home at Bucklersbury was a happy and busy home, but tightly disciplined. In many respects, Thomas ran it like a monastery. Idleness was not permitted. Besides their studies, the children all had chores to do, which included tending the garden and caring for a fairly large menagerie of animals. The evening meal began with a short reading, usually from Scripture, followed by an ordered conversation and finally merriment of some sort. There were both morning and evening prayers in which the entire household, including guests, joined, and the family followed the liturgical calendar. When it came to discipline, a little nagging from Alice and an occasional rebuke from Thomas seemed to do the trick. There were no punishments and Margaret Giggs, the adopted daughter, said that she sometimes would deliberately commit some fault so that she might enjoy Thomas's sweet and loving reproof. Thomas's daughter Meg said that she had seen her father angry only twice.

Throughout his life, Thomas understood that human beings were created to contemplate God and our purpose in life is to get to heaven. He taught that to his children. When one of them would complain about some discomfort or illness, he would remind her that no one can "go to heaven in feather-beds."

Since his family was wealthy by most standards, Thomas also taught his children never to consider money as their own. In a letter to Meg, he wrote:

> It is not a sin to have riches, but to love riches. "If riches come to you, set not your heart on them," says Holy Scripture.… He who forgets that his goods are the goods of God, and who reckons himself an owner rather than a disposer, takes himself to be rich. And because he reckons these riches to be his own, he casts his love on them and so much is his love set less upon God. For as Holy Scripture says, "Where your treasure is, there is your heart."

It's perhaps in the daily letters that Thomas exchanged with his children, well into their maturity, that his love for them came through. Those letters that survive are in *The Correspondence of Sir Thomas More*, by Elizabeth Rogers and published in 1947 by Princeton University Press. Thomas was careful not to neglect his son John, the only boy in a family of girls. The following letter shows that as well as the way he was careful to praise all of his children:

> Thomas More to his dearest children and to Margaret Giggs whom he numbers among his own.
> The Bristol merchant brought me your letters the day after he left you, with which I was extremely delighted.… So much does my affection for you recommend whatever you write to me. Indeed, without any recommendation, your letters are capable of

pleasing by their own merits, their wit and pure Latinity. There was not one of your letters that did not please me extremely; but to confess frankly what I feel, the letter of my son John pleased me best, both because it was longer than the others and because he seems to have given to it more labor and study. For he not only put out his matter prettily and composed in fairly polished language but he plays with me both pleasantly and cleverly, and turns my jokes on myself wittily enough. And this he does not only merrily, but with due moderation, showing that he does not forget that he is joking with his father, and that he is cautious not to give offense at the same time that he is eager to give delight.

Another letter from Thomas, this time only to his daughter Meg, shows the pride he had in his children as well as his love for them. It's a bit long, but worthy of quoting because it surely reveals the character of the writer as well as the recipient:

I will refrain from telling you, my dearest daughter, the extreme pleasure your letter gave me. You will be able to judge better how much it pleased your father when you learn what delight it caused to a stranger. I happened this evening to be in the company of his Lordship, John, bishop of Exeter, a man of deep learning and of a wide reputation for holiness. While we were talking, I took out of my desk a paper that bore on our business and by accident your letter appeared. He took it into his hand with pleasure and examined it. When he saw from the signature that it was a letter from a lady, he read it the more eagerly because it was such a novelty to him. When he had finished, he said he would hardly have believed it to have been your work unless I had assured him of the fact and he began to praise it in the highest terms (why should I hide what he said?) for its Latinity, its correctness, its erudition and its expressions of tender affection.

Seeing how delighted he was, I showed him your declamation. He read it and your poems as well, with a pleasure so far beyond what he had hoped that although he praised you most effusively, yet his expression showed that his words were all too poor to express what he felt. He took out at once from his pocket a gold coin which you find enclosed in this letter. I tried in every possible way to decline it but was unable to refuse to send it to you as a pledge and token of his good will towards you. This hindered me from showing him the letters of your sisters, for I feared that it would seem as though I had shown them to obtain for the others, too, a gift which it annoyed me to have to accept for you. But, as I have said, he is so good that it is a happiness to be able to please him. Write to thank him with the greatest care and delicacy. You will one day be glad to have given pleasure to such a man.

THE LAST FOUR THINGS

In 1522, Thomas proposed to Meg (some accounts say all of his children, but it probably was only Meg) that they each write an account of the four last things—death, judgment, hell and heaven, called *Quattuor Novissima*. It seems like a strange assignment because at the time Meg was a newlywed (she married at sixteen, the same age as her mother when she married Thomas) and was expecting her first child. It could be that he recalled that this was about the age when he became serious about spiritual matters.

The Four Last Things was not written for publication,

and it wasn't published during his lifetime. Besides, he never finished his treatise, not even the first part. But what he did write indicates what he wanted to teach to his eldest child and, undoubtedly, to her younger siblings. He began with the idea of pleasure, noting that people "are so set upon the seeking of pleasure that they set by pleasure much more than by profit." But he emphasized that "abandoning and refusing carnal pleasure while pursuing labor, travail, penance, and bodily pain will bring with it to a Christian—not only in the world to come, but also in this present life—real sweetness, comfort, pleasure, and gladness."

He wrote that it is important "to keep our minds occupied with good thoughts" because a "wandering mind" is never associated with "wisdom and good manners." Therefore, he wrote, "The active study of the four last things, and the deep consideration of them, is the thing that will keep you from sin."

He included a large section on the evil of pride, "the mischievous mother of all manner of vice." To overcome pride, he suggested imagining three scenarios.

First, a prince who is proud of his grand station in life, forgetting that death will take away all his royalty. He forgets, Thomas wrote, that soon he shall "have his dainty body turned into stinking carrion, be borne out of his princely palace, laid in the ground, and there left alone, where every lewd lad will be bold to tread on his head."

The second image was a stage on which everyone has a part to play. How foolish it would be, he wrote, for the person given a large part to get puffed up with pride. "Would you not laugh at his folly, considering that you are very sure that when the play is done he shall go walking as a knave in his old coat?"

The third image was that of a prison where some prisoners are bound to a post, some wandering about, some in a dungeon. Then they "are put to death in different ways in some corner of the prison, are thrown there in a hole, and are eaten either by worms under the ground or by crows above."

It's too bad that Thomas didn't finish his treatise. What we have is his contemplation of death and it would be interesting to have his thoughts about heaven. Nevertheless, we know that his purpose in writing, and in having Meg write, about the four last things was to enhance "the love of God and hope of heaven." This, he knew, was an essential part of the education of his children.

CHAPTER 3

LAWYER AND PUBLIC SERVANT

Yes, it is possible for a lawyer to become a saint, despite all the lawyer jokes in modern society. Perhaps it is as a lawyer and a public servant that Thomas serves most as a model for modern men and women. That's why he's the patron saint of lawyers, judges, politicians and statesmen and why Catholic lawyers belong to Saint Thomas More Societies. His decision to enter the king's service mirrors that of modern lawyers who often must give up lucrative salaries in order to serve the public.

Thomas More was not an ambitious man. That might sound like a ridiculous statement about a man who accomplished all that he did, but those who knew him best were sometimes frustrated by his refusal to promote himself. Undoubtedly the one who was most frustrated about that was his wife Alice. In his book *Dialogue of Comfort Against Tribulation*, Thomas reported this conversation with his wife:

> Alice asked, "What will you do since you do not wish to put yourself forth as other folk do? Will you still sit by the fire and make designs in the ashes with a stick as children do? Would God I were a man—look what I would do!"
> "Why, wife, what would you do?"

"What? By God, go forward with the best! Because, as my mother liked to say—God have mercy on
her soul—it is always better to rule than to be ruled.
And therefore, by God, I would never be so foolish
as to be ruled when I might rule."

"Here I must say that you have said the truth,
because I never found you willing to be ruled yet."

Whether or not Thomas was ambitious, he definitely had a
sense of duty. Perhaps that, as well as his unwillingness to remain
celibate, explains why he so willingly followed his father in the
practice of law instead of becoming a priest. He was admitted
to the bar in 1501 when he was twenty-three and it wasn't long
before he had a thriving practice. He soon earned a reputation
for his honesty and integrity. He wouldn't accept a case until
he had studied the matter thoroughly, warning his potential
clients that they must tell him the whole truth. Then, in most
cases, he tried to get the litigants to come to terms without
going to court. If that didn't work, he would show his clients
how to proceed at least expense. If he thought that justice was
on the side of his clients, he would argue the case forcefully,
and usually won. If he didn't think justice was on their side, he
would tell his clients so and advise them to give up the case.
If they insisted on continuing with it, he would refer them to
another lawyer.

In court, nobody could plead a case better. He knew the
law well and excelled at extemporaneous speech. His voice was
described as penetrating, but not loud. He articulated well and
spoke, it was said, neither hesitantly nor hurriedly.

He soon became Reader at Law at Furnivall's Inn, an inn
affiliated with his own Lincoln's Inn. He lectured there for
three years to an audience of clerks and other young attor-
neys. At Lincoln's Inn he was promoted to various positions of
responsibility—first to pensioner, or financial administrator, and
then in succession to butler, marshal and autumn reader—all

stages up the legal profession that successful lawyers in Tudor England were expected to follow. As autumn reader, he lectured for four mornings of four weeks on aspects of law, his lectures followed by discussion by the senior members of the inn. He served in this capacity twice, once in 1511 and again in 1516.

The Mercers' Guild was one of his biggest clients. Like his father before him, he was made a member, or a "freeman," of the guild. The Mercers customarily brought influential Londoners into its ranks, but Thomas was admitted because of his legal prowess. He worked with the guild as a negotiator and we know from documents the details of one such negotiation. It was with the chief magistrate of Antwerp, Belgium, and concerned the streets and buildings the English merchants could use in that city. As it happened, the magistrate, Jacob de Wocht, had already become a friend of Thomas's. In humanist circles (which we'll discuss in the next chapter) he was known as Jacobus Tutor. He had lived with Thomas for three months and dedicated his edition of Cicero's *De Officiis* to him.

According to the documents, the Mercers assembled in the hall and the magistrate and his delegation from Antwerp were summoned. Thomas opened the meeting with what was described as "a long and goodly proposition in Latin" on the business to be transacted. Then de Wocht replied in Latin, with Thomas translating into English what both had said for the assembled merchants. The negotiations continued in this way for several days until a settlement was reached, one that reportedly gave the Mercers everything they wanted in Antwerp.

PARLIAMENT, THEN UNDERSHERIFF

In both 1504 and 1510 Thomas was elected to Parliament. He didn't have to go through an election campaign though. Theoretically he was elected by the freemen of London, but in practice the representatives were chosen by the mayor, aldermen

and senior councilors. Thomas was chosen because of his work
with the Mercers, which was a powerful guild. The Parliament
of the early sixteenth century was not like that of today. It met
only when summoned by the king and it didn't meet between
1504 and 1510. The three hundred or so members of the House
of Commons met in Westminster Abbey from eight to eleven
in the morning over a period of four weeks; in the case of 1510,
from January 21 to the last week in February. (Thomas passed
his thirty-second birthday while Parliament was in session.) The
principal order of business was the granting of customs duties
to the king, who was now Henry VIII.

In the fall of 1510 Thomas was appointed one of two un-
dersheriffs of London, a position he later said he liked "better
than many others of higher rank." He continued in this post
for eight years. The three chief magistrates of the city, the lord
mayor and two sheriffs, were elected annually and usually were
merchants or businessmen, unskilled in law. The undersheriff,
therefore, advised them on legal issues. However, the position
also involved the responsibility of presiding as judge in the
sheriff's court.

Thomas carried out his work as judge every Thursday
morning. His court was at the Poultry Compter, a jail about
a five-minute walk from his home. There he dealt with every
kind of crime our modern city courts must handle—robberies,
rapes, assaults, arson, prostitution, etc. He experienced firsthand
the low life in London, not only in his courts, but in the streets
around his home—the taverns and bathhouses, public toilets
and barbers' shops, used by pimps, prostitutes, drunks, and
thieves, all swarming among the streets. Much later, in one of
his attacks on Martin Luther, he compared him to the whores
he met in his court who, when accused of some offense, would
shout "You're a liar!" He knew their kind well.

His work in the court took only a half-day a week, but he
was also legal advisor on various city bodies while continuing
his private legal practice. By the time Thomas reached his for-

ties, he had become the most successful lawyer in England. His son-in-law, William Roper, wrote that "there was at that time in none of the prince's courts of the laws of this realm, any matter of importance in controversy wherein he was not with the one party of council." Because of his reputation for integrity and prudent judgment, both as a lawyer and as a judge, his law practice grew enormously and he became quite wealthy. Roper said that he made four hundred pounds a year, equivalent to about eighty thousand dollars today—a substantial sum considering that the ordinary person lived on ten pounds a year. Thomas used his money for social, educational, and spiritual projects.

Thomas also made it a point to see the Archbishop of Canterbury, William Warham, every day. In fact, he was the first person to meet with him. We don't know much about their transactions, but the Church was the most powerful landowner and employer in England. Thomas continued his work with the Mercers, but also with the bakers and fishmongers. He appeared before the House of Lords at Westminster to speak on behalf of the London guilds over some matter. He negotiated with the Duke of Buckingham and the Bishop of Norwich over the rights of certain tradesmen to participate in city government. He was made commissioner of sewers, responsible for routine maintenance and the avoidance of flooding from the Thames. He also was a member of a commission charged with the maintenance of London Bridge, as his father was earlier. Thomas was a very busy man.

THE "EVIL MAY DAY" RIOTS

He was heavily involved in what came to be known as the "Evil May Day" riots of 1517. There had been epidemics of sickness in London and most people believed that they were brought there by foreigners, especially foreign merchants. Certain parties riled the people against these merchants and a report spread that there would be a riot on May Day and that all the foreigners would be murdered. As undersheriff, Thomas met with other city officials on April 30 to try to deal with the crisis. The council members decided on a curfew for the city and at 8:30 in the evening Thomas began to spread the order that no one could leave their homes until the next morning. But by this time it was too late. At eleven o'clock that night a crowd gathered. Thomas and other officials went out to meet them.

At this point legend and drama enter the story. In 1593, seventy-six years after the event, William Shakespeare and four other London dramatists wrote the play *Sir Thomas More*, which highly praised him. Evidence indicates that Shakespeare wrote the part about Thomas's role in the Evil May Day riots. According to his account, Thomas met the rioters and called out, "Good masters, hear me speak." The crowd quieted down enough for Thomas to make a speech calling for order and obedience. He told them that, if they ended up being banished as a result of what they planned to do, they themselves would be strangers in a foreign city. The crowd quieted down and dispersed.

Unfortunately, it didn't happen quite like that. It's true that Thomas and other officials met with the crowd and that Thomas spoke to them. It's true that he managed to calm the crowd —but only momentarily. Someone in the crowd hurled stones at the officials and a policeman shouted, "Down with them!" A full riot followed, violence and destruction continuing all night. Order wasn't restored until the next morning, after which three hundred men were arrested. The following Monday eleven of them were sentenced to be hanged. The rest of the three hundred, with halters around the necks, were led into the king's presence in Westminster Hall. Cardinal Thomas Wolsey, then Lord Chancellor of England, pleaded for their lives. At first King Henry VIII refused, but then relented. Thomas was present but said nothing.

TRAVEL OUTSIDE OF ENGLAND

Thomas had to travel outside of England on business on several occasions. He disliked this travel because it kept him away from his family for long periods of time. Of course, travel in the sixteenth century was far more difficult than it is today. Travelers often had to take their own beds with them, along with the food they planned to eat.

Thomas's first trip was to Bruges, Flanders. In 1515, he was asked to join an English mission to renegotiate commercial and diplomatic treaties between England and Flanders. The merchants of London were concerned because the regent of the Netherlands, Charles, had reached an agreement with France, England's enemy, and the English merchants were afraid that their ships might be seized and impounded. By this time Thomas had earned a reputation as a negotiator and an expert in commercial law, so the king's council, and presumably the London merchants, asked him to join the mission. The summons came with short notice but the city permitted a deputy to take over as undersheriff while he was away. His colleagues on the mission were Bishop Cuthbert Tunstall and Richard Sampson. Thomas also took John Clement, who married his adopted daughter, Margaret Giggs.

The party left London on May 12 and arrived in Bruges six days later—an indication of how long travel took. Of course, they went by ship. Then they had to wait for a couple weeks for Charles's commissioners to arrive. Once negotiations began, it became clear that the Netherlanders were in no hurry to sign an agreement. They deliberately misinterpreted previous treaties and refused to be exact in their demands. Thomas remained calm and firm, but negotiations were going nowhere, and they recessed for a while. As we will see in our next chapter, this is the time when Thomas used his forced idle time to start to write his masterpiece *Utopia*.

By the second week of July, when Thomas had thought

that negotiations surely would be finished, the delegation had to appeal to the king's council for more money. Thomas was unhappy, to say the least. He complained to Erasmus that he had to support himself in Bruges in the style customary for ambassadors of his country as well as his family back in England on less than a quarter of the income he would have earned if he were back in London. It was a complaint that countless statesmen would make thereafter.

Thomas was still in Flanders at the beginning of October, when he wrote to Richard Pace, Cardinal Wolsey's secretary, asking to be called back home because his role in the negotiations had become less significant. His request was granted and he returned home after an absence of five months. Later he declared that he was delighted by the results of the negotiations in Bruges.

In 1517 Thomas was again a member of a diplomatic mission, this time to Calais, England's outpost in France, to negotiate commercial disputes that had arisen between merchants in England and France. In addition, there were charges of piracy on the seas in cases where both countries appear to have been at fault. This time he was away from home for three months, from the beginning of September until the first part of December. He was in Calais when Martin Luther posted his ninety-five theses on the church in Wittenberg, Germany, an event that was to figure prominently in Thomas's future.

JOINING THE KING'S SERVICE

After he left Calais and before returning to England, Thomas rode to Bruges, where Richard Pace, now secretary to King Henry, was trying to create or finance a military alliance against France. Thomas undoubtedly had to report on his negotiations with France, but it seems that it was at this time that Thomas was being urged to enter the service of the king.

Pace undoubtedly tried to convince Thomas to become a royal councilor.

Thomas was reluctant. He understood well that service to the king would mean less time with his family—just as work in the U.S. White House today demands long hours. His children at the time ranged in age from thirteen to nine—just the time when he wanted to be with them to guide them in their formative years. During the years of his private practice and as undersheriff he was able to schedule his time so he could usually be at home most evenings, but that probably would no longer be possible. Service to the king would also mean less income for the family than he was able to make in private practice.

Besides, as we will see in the next chapter, Thomas wanted to write more. By the end of 1517 his writings had earned him a reputation as a Christian humanist. Erasmus definitely didn't want him to go into service to the king. Later, after Thomas did so, Erasmus lamented that Thomas's literary ambitions were "lost forever."

On the other hand, there were good reasons to join the king's service. Some of his humanist friends—Pace, Linacre and Tunstall, for example—were already serving on the king's council. In addition, in 1517 Pope Leo X issued a bull imposing a five-year truce among all Christian nations and Cardinal Wolsey had followed that up with a Treaty of Universal Peace. Perhaps, thought Thomas, this was an opportunity to do a great deal of good not only for England but for all of Christendom. Thomas believed that, as a councilor, he would be in a position to advise the king to follow his own best instincts.

Before joining the king's service, Thomas had a private meeting with Henry VIII. In a later letter, Thomas wrote that Henry told him to "look first to God and after God to him." This, he said, was "the first lesson that his Grace gave me when I first came into his noble service. Never could a king give his councilor or any other servant a more indifferent command or a more gracious lesson."

In 1518, Thomas took the first steps toward entering the king's service. In a letter to his friend Bishop John Fisher he wrote, "Much against my will did I come to Court—as everyone knows, and as the king himself in jest sometimes likes to reproach me. So far I keep my place there as precariously as an unaccustomed rider in his saddle."

His first duties consisted of hearing "poor men's suits." He and another councilor moved about from city to city listening to people who felt that they had been cheated or oppressed in some way. So Thomas traveled to courts in Windsor, Newhall, Hampton Court, Richmond, Abingdon, Woodstock, Southampton, Greenwich and Eltham, listening to complaints from those who didn't have the means to pay for a lawyer. His reputation for fair justice made him a logical choice for the position. He did that for a year before he was assigned other duties.

However, until the summer of 1519 Thomas wasn't paid. He had to present a petition to King Henry to correct what was apparently an oversight. Then Henry set his salary at one hundred pounds a year, backdated to the previous autumn. Thomas, though, waited until he received that payment before resigning his position as undersheriff.

We will return to Thomas's service for Henry VIII, but first we must consider his growing reputation as an author.

CHAPTER 4

A HUMANIST AUTHOR

Thomas might have been ahead of his time as a lawyer who also became an author. Some of our best fiction writers today are, or were, lawyers. He sometimes used his fiction as satire as a way to criticize his society, just as he would do later while defending the Catholic Church. Like all good writers, including modern authors, he seems to have had a compulsion to write, always turning to writing whether or not he hoped to have what he wrote published. Thus he's a model for modern writers.

Thomas More is known as a humanist. "Humanism" has had many definitions but in the early sixteenth century it connoted university teachers of the five humanities: grammar, rhetoric, poetry, history, and ethics. The sixteenth-century humanists liked to read the Greek and Latin classics to learn what it's like to be truly human and to put that into practice in their lives. Originally limited to those university teachers, it came to include their students who went on to other professions. Thomas More was one of those, as were the men who most influenced him—John Colet, William Grocyn, Peter Giles, Richard Pace, and Desiderius Erasmus, to name a few.

As we have seen, Colet was Thomas's first influence, his confessor and spiritual advisor, and the man who convinced him that his vocation was to marriage. Grocyn taught him Greek over a period of four or five years, among other things. We will note Giles' influence later in this chapter. Pace convinced him to enter service to the king. But perhaps Erasmus was the biggest influence on him.

We have already noted how Thomas and Erasmus met in 1499 and became friends. They communicated by mail frequently for the next five years before Erasmus returned to London in the spring of 1505, shortly after Thomas's wedding to Jane. When he returned in 1509, he stayed with the Mores for several months. As noted in Chapter 2, it was during that time that he wrote his most famous book *Encomium Moriae*. The Latin means *In Praise of Folly*, but with a slight shift it could mean "in praise of More," and indeed it was. Erasmus said that he wrote the book as a form of amusement while he was sick with lumbago, without any intention of publishing it. But after showing it to friends, he was encouraged to finish it, so he did so in seven days. It was a witty book that pierced the follies and abuses in both society and in the Church of the day. It made fun of lazy friars and greedy ecclesiastics as well as lawyers and scholastic theologians. It included jokes that Thomas and Erasmus shared.

Erasmus began the book with a letter to Thomas in which he called him the Democritus of a new age. Democritus was a fourth and fifth century B.C. Greek philosopher known as the Laughing Philosopher because he was wont to laugh at the follies of his age, and Erasmus thought of Thomas as constantly amused by the follies that surrounded him. This in itself tells us something of the cement that bound these two men together. They were both highly intelligent and learned and greatly enjoyed one another's wit and company.

It's from Erasmus's letters that we get the most complete picture of the man he called "the friend I love best." He wrote, "Whoever desires a perfect example of true friendship will seek it nowhere to better purpose than in More," and he described him as "born and made for friendship."

During Erasmus's three-month stay with Thomas, the two

men began a joint venture of translating the works of the Greek rhetorician and satirist Lucian from Greek to Latin. Lucian lived in the second century and most of his works were produced between 160 and 180. Thomas undoubtedly came across his works while studying Greek with Grocyn. In this venture, though, Thomas was the junior partner. He translated four of Lucian's dialogues while Erasmus provided twenty-eight. But in reading Lucian and translating his works, Thomas learned the possibilities of dialogue as a method of getting one's point across. His later works would assume that technique.

When published in 1506, the translation of Lucian's dialogues quickly became a best-seller among Europe's intelligentsia. We're not sure how many copies were sold but estimates of the number of editions range from nine to fourteen during Thomas's lifetime, more than his more famous book *Utopia*.

Travels with Thomas

Thomas made his first visit out of England in 1508, undoubtedly at the urging of Erasmus. He traveled to Paris and Louvain. Erasmus had taught at universities in both cities and had just recently spent two years at Louvain. It's possible that Thomas was able to combine some legal work for the London merchants on this trip, but the main purpose was to get to know some of the European scholars and humanists and to study the methods of teaching on the continent. With the success of the Lucian translations, he clearly thought of himself as one of the humanist scholars. Contacts at the centers of learning, such as Erasmus already had, couldn't hurt in the future.

Thomas's biographers also report on another trip because it was mentioned later in an important letter Thomas wrote to Martin Dorp, a theologian at Louvain. It was just a family visit to his sister Elizabeth in Coventry, England. She had married John Rastell, another lawyer who was then coroner of that city.

Later he would become a publisher and publish Thomas's book on the life of Pico della Mirandola. Although it was a relatively short trip, it still took three days by horseback.

Coventry was a city of extremely devout Catholics. It was famous for its Corpus Christi play (in which Rastell was also involved) that told the entire religious history of the world from creation through the Old Testament and ending with Christ's crucifixion and resurrection. As in London, there was a Carthusian Charterhouse and five churches. There, too, was a famous Hall of Saint Mary that was filled with tapestries celebrating the Blessed Virgin. There was also, at the time of Thomas's visit, a Franciscan friar who was preaching that anyone who recited the rosary every day was assured of salvation.

After his arrival, Thomas was asked what he thought about the friar's statement. He tried to laugh the matter off as ridiculous. But that night at dinner the friar appeared with some books about miracles and other divine interventions. He repeated his belief that anyone who recited the rosary every day could never be damned. Thomas again tried to treat the matter lightly but eventually replied that it seemed unlikely to him that anyone could purchase heaven at so little cost. He was laughed at. It seems similar to some Catholics today who believe that certain devotions to the Blessed Virgin, Saint Jude, or other saints, will guarantee their salvation. Thomas clearly believed that it takes more than prayers.

LETTER TO MARTIN DORP

As for that letter to Martin Dorp, it was a defense of Erasmus. Dorp criticized both Erasmus's *Praise of Folly* and his project of comparing the Vulgate translation of the New Testament with the original Greek text. Dorp thought that Erasmus's ridicule of people who held authority in the Church in *Praise of Folly* was dangerous and damaging to the Church.

As for Erasmus's translation of the New Testament into Latin, Dorp thought that it would downgrade the authoritative text of Saint Jerome's Latin translation. But besides that, Dorp also thought that pagan or secular studies were a threat to true piety, and humanists should stay away from the field of theology where they weren't qualified anyway.

Thomas, of course, was a layman who didn't claim to be a theologian, but he felt qualified to reply to Dorp's criticism, both as Erasmus's friend and as a humanist. It was more than just a personal dispute, though. If the faculty and the University of Louvain decided to condemn Erasmus's work, the new learning of the humanists might effectively be suppressed. Thomas's forty-seven page letter argued that humanists who knew Greek enough to go back to the original New Testament texts could only improve on the accuracy of Saint Jerome's Vulgate. He wrote that linguistic skills, such as a knowledge of Greek and Hebrew, were indispensable for biblical studies—far better than the debating skills of scholastic theologians. He called for what he called "positive theology," the type of pastoral teachings that the Fathers of the Church had practiced.

A true theologian, Thomas wrote to Dorp, was one who could comment and preach on biblical texts in a way that hearts could be moved and lives transformed, not one who used those texts in defense of a doctrinal position. The new humanist approach to theology, he said, was preferable to the medieval approach because it extended the palm of friendship rather than the clenched fist of disputation and argument.

As for that friar back in Coventry, Thomas criticized him for basing his devotional promises about the rosary on "a Mariale and from other books of that kind." He condemned those preachers who borrowed their sermons from the standard sermon manuals, because the sermon thus borrowed "is foolish in itself and when declaimed by a man more foolish still, how dull and stupid the whole affair becomes." He was not one to mince words.

Thomas sent the letter to Dorp, with a copy to Erasmus. It seems to have had the desired effect on Dorp, who withdrew his criticism. Erasmus was grateful to Thomas for writing the letter but urged him not to publish it for wider circulation. He didn't.

THE HISTORY OF RICHARD III

In 1513 Thomas began to write *The History of Richard III*. Almost eighty years later it would become the primary source of William Shakespeare's *Richard III*. However, we're not sure exactly why Thomas wrote it. It doesn't seem to have been written for publication of any kind and, indeed, one of the surviving manuscripts is prefaced with the statement that it was written for the sake of practice. It was at this time that Thomas was given permission to teach grammar at Oxford, so the explanation that it was a rhetorical and grammatical exercise seems plausible. Besides, he wrote it in both Latin and English, as he had his children do with their letters to him, although neither version is a direct translation of the other. He was still writing it when he entered King Henry VIII's service in 1518, at which time he discontinued it—perhaps for loss of interest, less time to devote to it, or because he thought it imprudent to continue.

Thomas's earliest biographers portrayed him as an avid reader of history, especially the Greek historians Thucydides and Plutarch and the Roman historians Sallust, Tacitus and Suetonius. In writing this history, or exercise, Thomas wrote in the style of some of these men, a mixture of narrative and long dramatically placed oration. We know that Thomas had recommended Sallust, a Roman historian who lived 86-34 B.C., to his children, and he evidently practiced what he preached.

This book, though, is "history" only in the loosest sense of the word—it's about an historical character during a fixed period of time. However, critics consider it more as drama, biography or propaganda. It reflected a theme that Thomas had considered for some time—tyranny and the corruption of good government. He had addressed the subject in some of his poems and Erasmus wrote that he "always had a special loathing for tyranny and a great fancy for equality."

The History of Richard III mainly concerns the events in England in 1483, after the death of King Edward IV. Thomas was a boy at the time and he was able to draw on many witnesses who were alive at the time, including, of course, his father. Richard had come to power through a mixture of guile and hypocrisy, eventually murdering the lawful king and his brother, Richard's nephews, in the Tower of London. Having obtained the crown, he became a tyrant who was knowingly and deliberately unjust. He then turned the country, which had had good government under Edward IV, into one with bad government.

Thomas raised the question: What should an individual do when he or she sees the erosion of civil liberties, as happened during the two-year reign of Richard III (he was killed in the Battle of Bosworth Field in 1485)? He said that most people do nothing: "They said that these matters are but kings' games, as it were stage plays, and for the most part played upon scaffolds, in which poor men are but onlookers. And they that are wise will meddle no farther. For they that sometimes step up and play with them, when they cannot play their parts, they disorder the play and do themselves no good."

His point was that Richard came to power only because no statesman stood up to stop him. Why, he asks, did no one see through Richard's deception and prevent the disappearance of the two legitimate heirs to the throne? His answer was that the political and ecclesiastical leaders at the time were only interested in currying favor with their new leader.

At one point in his history, Thomas includes a long digression to tell the story of Jane Shore, who had been King Edward IV's mistress. In the passage, Thomas acknowledges that "some will think this woman too insignificant a thing to be written about in the history of more important matters," but he does it anyway. One biographer, Peter Ackroyd, thinks that perhaps he composed it for his daughters. He notes that it might be based on Sallust's portrait of Sempronia in *Bellum Catilinae* since both women are called *docta*.

Thomas wrote that King Richard III, "playing the goodly, continent prince, clean and faultless in himself and sent from heaven into a vicious world to amend men's morals," ordered the bishop of London to make Jane Shore do public penance for her sexual sins by walking before a cross in a Sunday procession with a candle in her hand.

> So she walked with a countenance and carriage so demure and so womanly, even though out of all array save her kirtle only, and she looked so beautiful and comely, with a slight and unusual blush as the crowds were staring at her, that her humiliation won her much praise among those who were more attracted by her body than curious about the state of her soul. And many good folk that had disliked her in her living and were now glad to see her punished, were yet more sorry for her in her shame when they grasped that the Lord Protector had arranged it more from a corrupt intention than from any virtuous affection on his part.

The Writing of *Utopia*

In the previous chapter I wrote about Thomas's journey in 1515 to Bruges, in the Netherlands, and the long drawn-out negotiations over commercial treaties that kept him there from May to October. In July, when the Netherlands commissioners went to Brussels for further instructions in the negotiations,

Thomas rode to Antwerp. He stayed there with Peter Giles (or Gillis), a humanist friend of Erasmus and chief secretary to the city council. He remained there for six or seven weeks of unexpected leisure, during which he and Giles became close friends.

He also conceived the idea for the classic book we know today as *Utopia*. The word itself has come to mean an idealistic and impractical place of perfection or an unrealistic scheme for social reform. The full title of the book was *The Best State of a Commonwealth and the New Island of Utopia*. Thomas intended to contrast the society of Tudor England with the idealistic society he described in *Utopia*.

He wrote the book in Latin, clearly for Europe's intelligentsia. It wasn't translated into English until 1551, thirty-five years after it was originally published in Louvain in 1516 and sixteen years after Thomas's death. Once it was published, it was so well received that it was reprinted in Paris in 1517 and then two editions in Basle in 1518. The work is composed of two books. Thomas wrote the second book while he was in Antwerp and Bruges and the first book after he got back to England. Often people are content to read only Book Two, which describes life in Utopia, but Thomas obviously felt that the work wasn't complete without Book One, which describes life as Thomas knew it in England.

As is true of many of his books, this one consists mainly of dialogue. It begins in Antwerp, outside the cathedral church of Notre Dame. The fictitious character Thomas called Morus has just attended Mass. When he exits the church he finds his friend Peter Giles talking with a sunburned stranger with a long beard. He is introduced as Raphael Hythlodaeus, a Portuguese man who had traveled with Amerigo Vespucci to many parts of the world, including to the New World—only discovered twenty-three years earlier. Morus invites Hythlodaeus to his house (as we know, Thomas was really living with Giles at this time) to learn more about the man's travels.

Hythlodaeus first talks about a trip he made to England and a meal he had in the household of Archbishop Morton of Canterbury (where Thomas served table as a boy). The conversation soon concerned the ills of English society: capital punishment for minor crimes like theft, the large number of crippled war veterans among street beggars, the lifestyle of nobles who lived off the labor of the poor, and the growing disparity between the rich and the poor. Hythlodaeus said that he tried to offer some words of advice, but they fell on deaf ears. Therefore, he said, he had no interest in being a permanent counselor.

At this point, Morus says that Plato taught in *The Republic* that commonwealths would be happy only when philosophers became kings or kings became philosophers. If men like Hythlodaeus refuse to be counselors, "No wonder we are so far from happiness when philosophers do not condescend even to assist kings with their counsel." Hythlodaeus, though, insists that true philosophers must remain aloof from the corrupt world of politics. Further, he says, good government is impossible unless the evils of money and private property are eliminated, and people hold all goods in common. He knows this, he says, because, during his travels, he has seen a society where its citizens live in peace and happiness, where wealth is distributed evenly. Morus and Giles then suggest that they break for dinner (lunch to us moderns) before hearing more. Thus ends Book One.

Book Two begins with Hythlodaeus's travels with Amerigo Vespucci to the New World. He stayed behind for further exploration and came upon the island of Utopia, named for its founder, Utopus. Lo and behold, the geography of the island is the same as England and its capital city, Amaurotum, is identical to London. But the lives of the people are much different. Its properties are held in common; in fact, people exchange properties every ten years. There is no money, therefore no theft. There are no lawyers because there's no need for them. The people use gold and silver for chamber pots, not for jewelry, and the children play with gems. The people work six hours a day at the craft to which they are most suited, the rest of the time being devoted to intellectual pursuits or healthful recreation. They all wear the same simple clothing, with distinctions for gender and marital status. They eat in communal dining halls, the food coming from the common stock of a central market. It is, obviously, a description of a communist society.

Until recently, of course, the Utopians had never heard of Christianity. They tolerated different forms of religion but most of them believed "in a single power, unknown, eternal, infinite, inexplicable, far beyond the grasp of the human mind, and diffused throughout the universe, not physically but in influence." Most of them believed in the immortality of the soul. When the Utopians heard about Christianity after the discovery of the New World, they were well disposed toward it and many were baptized. But "those who have not accepted Christianity make no effort to restrain others from it, nor do they criticize new converts to it."

Naturally, Hythlodaeus tells much more about Utopia than I have room for here, including its enlightened government, social relations, travel restrictions, and their search for happiness. He ends his description by comparing "this justice of the Utopians with that which prevails among other nations," and says that he can see in those other nations "nothing but a conspiracy of the rich, who are fattening up their own interests under the name and title of the commonwealth."

Morus, though, remains very suspicious of Hythlodaeus's cure: Utopian communism. When he tries to respond, Hythlodaeus becomes somewhat touchy, so Morus suggests they put the matter aside for another day and leads him in for supper. Morus concludes, "While I can hardly agree with everything he said… yet I freely confess that in the Utopian commonwealth there are many features that in our own societies I would like, rather than expect, to see."

In writing the book, Thomas seems to have used various sources, but especially Plato, whom he mentions seven times in the book itself and four times in accompanying letters. Plato's *The Republic* was also a scheme for an ideal society. Other sources might have been Macrobius, Aristotle, Seneca, Lucian, Cicero, Saint Augustine, and, of course, the Acts of the Apostles that says that the early Christians held everything in common.

Utopia has been widely discussed ever since Thomas wrote it. Did he believe that such a society as he described was desirable? His final statement, quoted above, probably indicates his beliefs about the matter. But so do the names in the book. "Utopia," for example, means "nowhere." The protagonist is Raphael Hythlodaeus. Raphael was the name of the archangel who guided Tobiah in the Book of Tobit, but Hythlodaeus means one who is cunning in nonsense or idle gossip. Hythlodaeus also said that he traveled with Amerigo Vespucci. In 1515 it was believed that his accounts of his voyages were fabrications and in no way truthful, so it wasn't a compliment for Thomas to say that Hythlodaeus was Vespucci's companion. Furthermore, there are numerous ambiguities throughout the book that I don't have room here to point out.

The final consensus is that *Utopia* is one of the most elaborate and successful exercises in satire ever to have been composed. John Ruskin described it as "perhaps the most really mischievous book ever written." It was destined to inspire numerous later satirical and "utopian" books. Only a few examples include these: Tomasso Campanella's *City of the Sun*, written in 1623, is a utopia built around a society led by the Catholic hierarchy. Francis Bacon's *New Atlantis*, in 1626, stresses the role of technology in bringing about the happiness of society. James Harrington's *Oceana*, 1656, elaborates a political utopia in the form of a romance. Jonathan Swift's *Gulliver's Travels*, 1726, and Aldous Huxley's *Brave New* World, 1932, are the most famous of the utopian satires, and George Orwell's *1984*, written in 1949, would also fit the category.

It wasn't until the summer of 1516 that Thomas was able

to complete Book One. Erasmus had visited him earlier that year and stayed with him briefly, but this was the visit already mentioned in which he realized that Alice More wasn't pleased to be caring for him, so he moved out after a couple weeks. Nevertheless, the two men obviously discussed Thomas's book during that visit and made plans for its publication.

The completed manuscript arrived in Erasmus's home in Antwerp three weeks after his return from London, along with a letter to Peter Giles that became the dedicatory letter to the book. At that point the book was titled *Nusquama* ("Nowhere") and it was apparently Erasmus who suggested changing the title to *Utopia*. Erasmus edited the manuscript and then supervised every stage of its preparation and publication, including the printing done in Louvain. He also collected letters from other humanists among his friends in order to give the book a good send-off among humanists. The book was published at the end of 1516, became an immediate success, and cemented Thomas's reputation as a humanist author.

FOUR LETTERS ON HIGHER EDUCATION

The humanists were particularly concerned about education, and for Thomas that meant not only the education of all the members of his family but higher education, too. His ideas about higher education were clearly expressed in four letters. We already mentioned the one he wrote to Martin Dorp at Louvain in 1515. He wrote the other three after he began to serve King Henry VIII.

The first was to Oxford University, in 1518. Some of the faculty there began to call themselves "Trojans" because they were opposed to "Greeks," that is, those who wanted to teach Greek and the liberal arts. They favored what had come to be orthodox scholastic teaching. Thomas felt called on to compose a lengthy letter to the proctors and masters of the university defending the teaching of secular letters as a way of advancing true knowledge and virtue. He attacked the unnamed "Trojan" preacher and urged the university authorities to end the factions that were attacking the liberal arts.

In this regard, Thomas had the support of King Henry, Cardinal Wolsey (the Archbishop of York and Lord Chancellor), and William Warham (Archbishop of Canterbury). According to Erasmus, there was a later sequel to this episode when a theologian preached before King Henry and attacked the study of Greek, obviously unaware of the king's support for such learning. The king was said to have first smiled at his secretary, Richard Pace, and then asked Thomas to debate with the theologian. After Thomas gave a masterful talk, the theologian knelt before the king and begged to be excused from making a reply. The theologian never returned to the court.

The second and third of Thomas's humanist letters after he began service to the king were to a monk named John Batmanson and to Richard Lee, who later would become Archbishop of York. He wrote them in 1519. Batmanson had been in the Carthusian Charterhouse when Thomas was living there, and he had been acquainted with Lee for many years. The issue in this case was Erasmus's translation of the New Testament. In *Novum Testamentum*, he had published parallel Greek and Latin texts and many theologians looked on this as an act of impiety.

Besides defending Erasmus, though, Thomas attacked Batmanson, describing him at one point as an ignorant and unknown little monk with a foul tongue. He also attacked some aspects of monasticism as, perhaps, only one who has experienced the life could do. He excoriated those who preferred to stay in one place "like a sponge," and try to escape the troubles of the world. It was not one of Thomas's better efforts.

There was still another letter that deserves attention at this point. It was written in 1520 to Germanius de Brie, known as Brixius. It was an attempt by Thomas to defend something he had brought on himself. Back in 1513 Thomas had written some unflattering verses about Brixius in a poem concerning a sea battle between two nations, accusing the Frenchman of false heroics. Thomas published the verses in his *Epigrammata* in 1518 and Brixius saw them. In response, Brixius published his *Antimorus*, a long poem followed by prose commentary. He attacked Thomas's skills as a grammarian and rhetorician, calling him a "moron," a pun on his name. In the prose commentary, he pointed out some errors in Thomas's Latin verses, saying that he really should learn the language properly. It was an attack of one humanist on another.

But *Antimorus* also put Thomas in some danger. Brixius recalled a celebratory poem Thomas had written when Henry VIII became king (which I'll mention again in the next chapter), and said that he was astonished that Thomas would have chosen to denounce the previous king, Henry's father. If Henry VIII realized what Thomas had written, Brixius said, "I am afraid for you."

Thomas recognized the threat for what it was, so he quickly replied with a long and strong letter to Brixius. He backtracked from some of his earlier remarks about Henry VII, saying that some of his counselors took advantage of his sickness. Then he mounted another attack on Brixius, accusing him of plagiarism and fabrication of the truth. He preached to him about his breach of decorum and said that he was bringing humanism into disrepute.

By this time, Thomas was being more careful about what he wrote because of his position in the king's service. He asked one scholar not to publish their correspondence until he had time to revise it. He deleted some of his poems from a later edition of *Epigrammata*, substituting a new letter in verse to his children, expressing his love for them. Thomas was now a politician and had to be careful about his private life and his reputation.

CHAPTER 5

POLITICIAN AND STATESMAN

Foreign policy can often be messy. It should be obvious that a negotiator for a government must try to achieve what is best for that government, and Thomas did that successfully. He also sought peace through the treaties he negotiated. When peace wasn't always possible, he performed his duties and responsibilities to the best of his abilities. Modern politicians and statesmen face similar situations and they could benefit by looking for help from Saint Thomas More.

Thomas was thirty-one when Henry VIII became king in 1509 at the age of seventeen. Thomas and most of the other people in England were happy, and Thomas composed a Latin poem that celebrated Henry VIII's coronation. In the poem he alluded to the atmosphere of fear and suspicion that existed during the reign of Henry VII, but he particularly celebrated the new golden age that the people envisioned. The young Henry VIII was known as handsome and athletic, as well as pious and learned, and Thomas's poem rejoiced in all that. As a prominent lawyer, Thomas was already well acquainted with many members of the king's court, but he didn't join them officially for another nine years, in 1518.

He was, as noted in Chapter 3, frequently associated with the king's court. Ever since 1516, it's said, he was always present to greet Cardinal Wolsey, the Lord Chancellor, the first thing every morning. He was obviously cultivating the second most powerful man in England. He even wrote two Latin poems to him as the bountiful father, and it appears that he really believed that Cardinal Wolsey was the best chance for reform in both the Church and the state. He had been on diplomatic missions in the company of Richard Pace, the cardinal's secretary, and, as noted, it was he who finally convinced him to enter the service of the king. He professed his reluctance to Erasmus but there are reasons to doubt that he was really that reluctant.

In Chapter 3 we saw that his first duties involved hearing "poor men's suits," moving about from city to city listening to people who felt that they had been cheated or oppressed in some way. By 1519, though, he was the king's second secretary. Since the first secretary, Richard Pace, was frequently out of the country on secret diplomatic business, it fell to Thomas to be the regular mediator of the correspondence between King Henry and Cardinal Wolsey. He would be called into the king's presence and Henry would dictate what he wanted Thomas to write. He would then write the letter and present it to the king for his signature. He would also read aloud the communications received from Cardinal Wolsey. It's what was done before the days of e-mail, or, for that matter, before the days of the type-writer. It did, however, seem somewhat below the talents of a man like Thomas, and it kept him working late into the night.

It wasn't long before Thomas became trusted by both of the two most powerful men in England. Letters between them concerned matters of war, since England was about to wage war against France. Apparently Thomas was careful not to interject his own opinions unless he was asked for them and he was also always courteous to the king and the cardinal-lord chancellor.

As royal secretary, he gradually became more powerful. Members of the King's Council knew that the best way to reach the king was by writing to Thomas. He also dealt with foreign ambassadors. He kept the codes for secret correspondence with diplomats, and he read the first drafts of treaties or diplomatic instructions. His role continued to expand when he was given control of the king's signet seal, by which he made various forms of state expenditures. He was a member of the King's Council and was appointed to various commissions. When the king traveled, Thomas was always at his side. In March and April of 1518, for example, the king moved from place to place outside of London in order to escape another attack in London of the plague and sweating sickness. Thomas was undoubtedly concerned about his family, living in the middle of London, but he remained at the side of the king.

BEING MERRY WITH KING AND QUEEN

While at court, Thomas was not only with Henry during the day, but was also frequently invited to join him and Queen Catherine for dinner. William Roper wrote that Thomas would often "sit and confer" with Henry and, after dinner, would "be merry" with both the king and queen, never forgetting the usual formulas of courtesy. Roper also told of the king taking Thomas to the roof of the palace to discuss the movements and operation of the stars. All this, of course, indicates that Thomas was being forced by his responsibilities to spend much less time with his family.

On the other hand, his position also gave him the opportunity to help his extended family in other ways—ways that were deemed acceptable in those days and, indeed, taken for granted. Thomas's father, John More, was knighted in 1518 and in 1520 was appointed to the King's Bench, which might or might not have happened if Thomas wasn't the king's counselor. John Rastell, Thomas's brother-in-law, moved from Coventry to London, where he established himself as a printer and bookseller in a favorable location. As he had done in Coventry, he arranged pageants for the city, and he also played a prominent part in building English fortifications in France. Rastell's son-in-law, John Heywood, who married Thomas's niece, became a groom of the royal household. Rastell and Heywood were the first known English dramatists.

During this time, two kings—Henry VIII of England and Francis I of France—and an emperor—Charles V, Holy Roman Emperor as well as the ruler of Spain and Burgundy—were involved in complex disputes. To complicate matters more, Charles was the nephew of Henry VIII's wife, Catherine of Aragon. In 1520, Thomas was one of a small group responsible for negotiating with representatives of Emperor Charles various diplomatic and commercial matters. From that negotiation he quickly became a member of Henry's entourage to Calais, France for negotiations with King Francis.

This negotiation has come to be known as the Field of Cloth of Gold. Both kings were arrayed in elaborate golden clothing, so dazzling, it was said, that it was hard to gaze on them. They met in a valley, approaching each other with a retinue of more than two thousand men. Each pavilion, one for the English and one for the French, was decorated with richly painted cloth. Cardinal Wolsey said a High Mass. It was a great spectacle denoting peace.

After the negotiations at Calais were completed, Thomas and some other counselors moved on for other negotiations at Bruges, a city he was beginning to know well. The negotiations there, though, didn't go smoothly and continued for some seven or eight weeks. By the time Thomas was able to return to London, he had been gone for almost three months. Still more time away from his family.

KNIGHTED AS SIR THOMAS MORE

In 1521, Thomas was promoted to the lucrative position of under-treasurer, charged with supervising the work of the British Exchequer. In this role, he was responsible for recording the collection and disbursement of England's treasury as well as for handling the costs and expenses of the king and his court. According to custom, this position came with knighthood, so Thomas was duly knighted and became Sir Thomas More. King Henry called him "our trusty and well beloved counselor Thomas More, now knight." He was now expected to wear his chain of knighthood and, while riding, golden spurs.

His salary was the second highest in the Exchequer, but it was only part of his income. As a favorite servant of the king, he received enough grants and favors to at least double his remuneration. Even before becoming under-treasurer he was given half of the revenue for the royal exchanger, the one who controlled the exodus of bullion from England. Other sources of income included a license he received to export woolen cloths, a license he then sold to a merchant; an annual retainer from the Earl of Northumberland; payments from a bishop and a lord; a pension from the king of France; and various sums from the Mercers. By this time he had given up most of his private law practice, but he still did some work for the Mercers, including, in 1522, arranging protection for a fleet of merchant ships traveling from the Netherlands.

He also received a considerable amount of property: Henry gave him the manors of Doglington and Fringeford, and some property in Oxfordshire. In 1522, he received the manor of South in Kent that had belonged to Edward, the Duke of Buckingham, who the previous year had been charged with treason, convicted, and beheaded on Tower Hill. He was severely criticized for taking lands from the estate of a man who had been executed for treason, even though there is no evidence that he had anything to do with the execution. Here is what Peter Ackroyd wrote about this in his *The Life of Thomas More*:

> He was not averse to profiting from some, if not all, of these enviable possessions. Here we come close to one of the complexities of More's life and career. He lived in the spiritual world as well as the secular

world. In the former he practiced individual prayer and penitence, while in the latter he derived his identity from the social hierarchy in which he found himself. One was a question of private, the other of customary, ritual. To be a good Christian, in both worlds, required obedience and the fulfillment of obligations—which included providing an inheritance for his descendants.

Thomas More was becoming a very wealthy man.

Involvement in Foreign Policy

Even while he was under-treasurer, Thomas was getting more and more involved in foreign policy. Less than a year after his previous trip to Bruges, he was back again, once more to negotiate with the merchants there. But before he finished his work there, King Henry ordered him to Calais to join Cardinal Wolsey who was supposedly trying to resolve a conflict between France and the Holy Roman Empire. In a message to Wolsey, the king told him to make Thomas "privy to all such matters as your Grace shall treat at Calais." Those "matters" concerned a secret treaty that Wolsey was trying to arrange with Emperor Charles that, if negotiations for peace with France failed, would result in a joint invasion of France by the empire and England.

In August of 1521, Wolsey and Thomas went back to Bruges to meet with Charles's representatives. When Wolsey returned to Calais for negotiations with the French, Thomas remained in Bruges to negotiate with Charles's representatives. Erasmus was a member of the emperor's delegation, so the two friends enjoyed seeing one another. They didn't realize it at the time, of course, but this was the last time the two friends would meet.

Thomas rejoined Wolsey in Calais in September. In October he was sent back to England to report directly to King

Henry. Unfortunately, he arrived in London with a severe fever, feeling both hot and cold all over his body at the same time. His doctors were baffled by those and other symptoms and were having trouble treating his illness. Then Margaret Giggs, his adopted daughter who, as noted in Chapter 2, had been one of the first women in England to study medicine, remembered reading about his condition. A remedy was found and Thomas was recovered by the middle of November.

The negotiations in Calais, ostensibly mediation between the Holy Roman Empire and France, eventually broke down, and England prepared for war against France. Thomas was involved in a survey of England's financial and military resources. He was also responsible for preparing for the internment of French enemy aliens.

Emperor Charles V arrived in London in June of 1522 to conclude the treaties that Thomas had been negotiating in Bruges the previous year. There was a grand welcoming ceremony for him and Thomas was chosen to deliver an eloquent oration in praise of both the emperor and King Henry and the "comfort it was to their subjects to see them in such amity." For the occasion, he even purchased a velvet gown.

SPEAKER OF THE HOUSE OF COMMONS

As part of the preparations for war, Henry convoked Parliament in 1523, mainly for the purpose of raising money for the invasion of France. Thomas was formally "elected" Speaker of the House of Commons, although there was never any doubt that he was there as the king's servant. Once again, as happened throughout his career, Thomas accepted, but did not seek, a high office. In his opening address, he made a plea for freedom of speech among the members of Parliament. This was at least two centuries before freedom of speech was recognized as a human right.

Thomas was now a politician for sure. His task was to

convince the members of Parliament to grant the funds the king wanted, and many members were not willing to do so. Cardinal Wolsey, as Lord Chancellor, spoke at the opening session and demanded that a large sum be appropriated to guard "the king's honor and the reputation of this realm" by keeping the promise he had made to Charles V and prosecuting the war against his "ancient enemy, the French king." However, as politicians are often known to do, the members of Parliament procrastinated and tried to appropriate a smaller amount.

Two weeks later, Wolsey returned, this time with a large retinue. He berated the members and began to demand of individual members what their response was. Finally, Thomas fell on his knees before the Lord Chancellor and begged that his colleagues be excused because it "was neither expedient nor agreeable with the ancient liberty of the house" for them to debate with him. Wolsey left without the matter being settled. Thomas then used all his skills as a negotiator and politician. Eventually, the House of Commons voted a large sum to the king. Wolsey and Thomas got what they needed.

Wolsey was so pleased with the result, and Thomas's role, that he asked the king to reward him with an extra grant of one hundred pounds, double the conventional fee for the Speaker. Besides that, in 1524, Wolsey appointed Thomas High Steward of Oxford University and the next year gave him the same position at Cambridge University. These were not academic appointments, but rather judicial and financial. Besides being concerned with the universities' business affairs, he was involved in trying serious offenders within the jurisdiction of the universities. Naturally, he was well paid for his efforts.

He was using much of his income to buy property. In 1523, while Parliament was in session, he bought Crosby Place and adjoining grounds for one hundred fifty pounds. Crosby Place was described as a very large and beautiful house, the highest at that time in London. Thomas purchased the house from a former lord mayor of London named John Rest, and then sold it eight months later for two hundred pounds to Antonio Bonvisi, an Italian merchant and good friend. Bonvisi then turned around and leased the house to William Roper and William Rastell. The reasons for these elaborate transactions are not clear, but Bonvisi might have been paying Thomas indirectly for services rendered.

Thomas also bought twenty-seven acres of land in Chelsea for thirty pounds and more than seven acres of land in Kensington for twenty pounds. As we will see later, he was to build his great house in Chelsea.

SOME DEVIOUS NEGOTIATIONS

After Parliament adjourned in 1523, and Thomas's duties as Speaker were over, he returned to King Henry's side. War had now started, and England invaded France. Henry was determined to defeat Francis I of France as his father had defeated Richard III. The Duke of Suffolk was leading the English troops. They came within seventy miles of Paris, but couldn't get any farther and eventually had to retreat to Calais. Henry obviously hadn't achieved his objective, but he resigned himself to the facts and ordered Thomas to engage in secret negotiations for peace.

In 1524, a friar named John Joachim, supposedly from Genoa, Italy, arrived in London and stayed with Antonio Bonvisi at Crosby Place. Thomas was one of the few people who knew that Joachim was really there to arrange a secret treaty between England and France. Needless to say, such a treaty would be in direct contradiction to the terms of England's treaty with Charles V.

Thomas was involved in other devious measures, too. At one point, the ambassador from the Holy Roman Empire to England sent a courier with letters to the emperor. English authorities detained him and took the letters to Thomas's home.

Thomas read them and then sent them on to Cardinal Wolsey. Duplicity was rampant on all sides.

At the beginning of 1525 imperial troops won the Battle of Pavia, Italy, against French troops. Some eight thousand of them were killed and King Francis was captured. Naturally, there was rejoicing in England, but then Emperor Charles refused to support England. Henry knew that it was time to make peace with France, so he sent Thomas to negotiate the final treaty with France. He signed the treaty in the summer of 1525.

Biographers have long questioned Thomas's motives during the events leading up to the war, and the war itself. How much was he involved in making policy and how much was he simply obeying the orders of his superiors, King Henry and Lord Chancellor Wolsey? Evidence indicates that he wanted peace, but he apparently also thought it important, for the sake of peace, for England to exert a strong presence in the politics of Europe.

CHANCELLOR OF THE DUCHY OF LANCASTER

At the end of the summer of 1525, as the peace treaty with France was signed, Cardinal Wolsey offered Thomas the position of Chancellor of the Duchy of Lancaster. That position had been filled by Sir Richard Wingfield, but he died. Thomas accepted the position and resigned as England's under-treasurer. The duchy's estates, in which about forty thousand people lived, lay to the north and west of London, but Thomas didn't have to visit there often. His principal responsibility as chancellor was to preside at the Court of the Duchy Chamber located in an upstairs room of Westminster Hall in London.

For the next four years he heard cases that were similar to those he had heard while he was undersheriff of London: theft, murder, arson, trespass, and suits over the ownership of land. During that time, he enhanced his reputation as a fair judge, more concerned about getting to the causes of violence than to inflict punishment, a protector of the weak against the strong, and a hardworking administrator who could cut through a mass of details to get to the heart of the matter.

Even though Thomas now had these duties as Chancellor of the Duchy of Lancaster, he was still called upon for diplomatic duties. In 1527, Charles V and his Holy Roman Empire were on the rampage again, forcing England and France closer together. Thomas was one of the central figures in negotiating still another treaty with France, which he signed at the end of April. To celebrate, Henry sponsored a jousting tournament followed by a great banquet and ball on May 6.

Unknown to the participants, on that same day Charles's imperial forces ransacked Rome and committed atrocities that wouldn't be forgotten for decades, or more. The troops disemboweled old men, castrated young men, raped women, and threw children onto the points of swords. Pope Clement VII fled to Castel Sant'Angelo while the mob dragged the corpse of Pope Julius II from its ornate tomb and paraded it around the streets of Rome. When word of this reached England, it made Henry VIII even more determined to form an alliance with France against the emperor.

So, in July of 1527, Cardinal Wolsey, Thomas and a great many others traveled to France to solemnly ratify the treaty that Thomas had negotiated. Having reached France, the entourage took weeks to travel from Calais to Amiens, with public processions and festivities in all the towns they passed through. In August, the treaty was finally solemnized in the cathedral at Amiens. Thomas didn't return to England until late September.

THE TREATY OF CAMBRAI

However, this treaty, too, didn't hold for long. In 1529, Francis I of France and Emperor Charles were obviously moving toward a separate peace that would exclude England. By that time Wolsey was embroiled in Henry's efforts to get his marriage to Catherine annulled (as we'll see in a later chapter), so he couldn't travel outside of England. In June, Thomas and Bishop Cuthbert Tunstall, along with two other envoys, were sent to Cambrai, which then was part of the Holy Roman Empire, to do what they could in a difficult situation. The main objective was to ensure that debts owed by the empire to Henry would continue to be paid and that trade between England and the Low Countries wouldn't be threatened.

They were tough negotiations, with many frustrations and deliberate delays. Eventually, though, Thomas was able to negotiate separate agreements with all the parties and, at the beginning of August, a general peace was proclaimed. The peace was to last for fifteen years—a long time in those days. Thomas was so satisfied by the results that this diplomatic mission is the only public event that he chose to commemorate on the tombstone in the church in Chelsea where he expected some day to be buried. His epitaph notes this time "when the leagues between the chief Princes of Christendom were renewed again and peace so long looked for [was] restored to Christendom."

When Thomas returned to London from Cambrai, he found that Cardinal Wolsey had fallen out of favor with Henry VIII because of his failure to obtain for him an annulment of his marriage to Catherine. We'll get into the details of that effort in a later chapter, but here we can note that Thomas was surely aware of the king's growing dissatisfaction with his Lord Chancellor. On October 9, Wolsey was indicted for praemunire (an offense against the English Crown) and arrested for treason. Later that month he surrendered the Great Seal, loudly lamenting his fate.

On October 25, 1529, King Henry VIII appointed Sir Thomas More Lord Chancellor of England.

CHAPTER 6

AT HOME IN CHELSEA

Thomas's children, grandchildren and pets were certainly rambunctious. His home sounds like a twenty-first century home (without the conveniences). There is much that modern parents can emulate in Thomas's life at home in his large house at Chelsea. Perhaps we don't own as large a home as he did, but we can still enjoy our children and grandchildren as he did. And Thomas also gave us a good example of how to be a good neighbor.

It was at about the time that he was appointed Chancellor of the Duchy of Lancaster that Thomas was also deeply involved in the plans for his new house. As already noted, he bought twenty-seven acres (some accounts say thirty-four acres) of farmland at Chelsea, then located two miles from London on the Thames River, in 1523. One could travel there by horseback or, more easily, by barge and rowboat on the Thames. Sometime in 1525, or perhaps early in 1526, after living in Bucklersbury for twenty years, Thomas moved his family to Chelsea. He was now forty-eight years old and his children started to have their own children—eleven grandchildren were born before More was imprisoned—and he liked them to be together.

The home at Chelsea has been called spacious rather than magnificent. Built of Tudor red-brick, it measured one hundred sixty-four feet across the front, with a porch and two bays, with two sets of windows on either side. It was large enough to accommodate the families of his four children as well as friends who would visit. One biographer says that Thomas may have been supporting as many as forty people—his family, in-laws, grandchildren, stepchildren, foster children, tutors, servants and secretaries—although they might not all have been living with him. His son-in-law, Giles Heron, managed the estate for him.

If we approached the house from the river, as Thomas usually did when he arrived home by barge, we would first walk through one of two gates that led to spacious gardens filled with a variety of trees and flowering shrubs. There was an orchard with apples, pears, plums and apricots, and spreading grape vines. The path through the gardens led to the front porch and then directly into the interior. Wooden screens were on the right side, protecting the great hall. The family ate their meals at one end of the great hall on a raised dais. The room itself was more than seventy feet in length and rose up to the beamed and timbered roof. A door by the raised dais led to the chapel and the staircase to the upper floor where the bedrooms and studies were located. The kitchen, pantry and servants' quarters were all on the left side of the house.

However, in a large family there is such a thing as too much togetherness, so Thomas also had constructed a building at the corner of his property, fairly distant from his busy home, that housed his private chapel, library and gallery. There he retired to study, pray and write—sometimes, especially on Fridays, for the whole day. He later wrote, "It is necessary for a man to choose himself some secret solitary place in his own house as far from noise and company as he conveniently can, and there let him sometime secretly resort alone imagining himself as one going out of the world." Here, too, away from his family, Thomas scourged himself with a leather thong.

A church built in the twelfth century, dedicated to All Saints, was near Thomas's estate. He greatly enlarged it shortly after moving to Chelsea; his coat-of-arms and crest carved in the chapel bear the date 1528. He restored the vault of the chapel and brought his first wife's remains there, expecting to be buried there himself. As he did in the church across the road from his home in Bucklersbury, he frequently served at Mass and sang in the choir. It's reported that the Duke of Norfolk once criticized him for performing such a humble role as altar server and Thomas replied, "My master the king cannot be displeased at the service I pay to his master, God."

A similar story was told concerning his participation in parish processions. Because of his rank as knight, he was offered a horse, but he replied, "My Lord went on foot. I will not follow him on horseback."

Thomas was also a good neighbor. It's known that he visited the poor in Chelsea, giving some of his money. An early biographer, Thomas Stapleton, says that he established a separate house for the poor, the infirm and the elderly. His daughter Meg supervised the house.

When he was home, he followed a routine similar to that while he lived at Bucklersbury. He tried to go to bed at nine o'clock at night so he could get up at two in the morning to say his prayers, study and write. He attended seven o'clock Mass and then began the duties of the day, usually traveling by barge to London. If he was able to get home early enough, the entire household joined him in evening prayers, which included the seven penitential psalms (six, thirty-two, thirty-eight, fifty-one, one hundred two, one hundred thirty, and one hundred forty-three) and the Litany of the Saints. At meals, at least when Thomas was home, someone would first read a passage from Scripture. That would then be the subject of conversation. Thomas was disinterested in food and ate sparingly, usually the first dish put before him and nothing else. When home, he fasted on Fridays.

The Family Portrait by Holbein

Shortly after the More family moved to Chelsea, Thomas commissioned the German master painter Hans Holbein the younger to paint a formal portrait of his family. Holbein stayed with the Mores on and off until sometime in 1528, so he came to know the family well. He painted the portrait in 1527. A preliminary sketch of that painting still exists; Thomas sent it to Erasmus after the oil portrait was completed and it is now in the Kunstmuseum in Basle, Switzerland. However, the painting itself, which measured approximately one hundred by one hundred forty inches, was destroyed in the mid-eighteenth century. Another painted version, not as good as the Holbein original, was completed at the end of the sixteenth century. In 1995, to commemorate the four hundred sixtieth anniversary of Thomas's death, the Thomas More Society of Dallas commissioned a smaller painting based on Holbein's sketch.

The unique painting, considered the first example of an intimate group of a non-ceremonial kind in northern Europe, shows the family gathered together, perhaps for evening prayers. Since it's a formal portrait, they are wearing formal attire. Yet there are also informal aspects in the painting, for example, books scattered on the floor and even a monkey crawling up Alice's dress. (In the version painted at the end of the sixteenth century, a dog lies at Thomas's feet, but it's not in Holbein's sketch.) The background shows fine woodwork and wall hangings, a lattice window on the right side, and freshly cut flowers on ornate cupboards. A clock, a new invention at the time (it would have had only an hour hand), hangs near the middle of the picture, and there are musical instruments on the left side.

Thomas, of course, is seated in the middle of the painting, his hands hidden by the sleeves of his black velvet cloak that has a brown fur collar. (Another portrait of Thomas by Holbein, now in the Frick Collection in New York, shows his hands, a ring on one of the fingers of his left hand and his right hand holding a piece of paper.) He is wearing his gold chain, indicating his knighthood. He has a broad forehead, a lean face, a large nose, thin lips, and a short neck. (In the other portrait, he also has a two-day growth of beard, for some unknown reason.) He is wearing a black cap with flaps down the side, but sideburns to the bottom of his ears are visible. (The painting doesn't show more of his hair but a larger-than-life bronze statue of Thomas in Chelsea, unveiled by the Speaker of the House of Commons in 1969, shows him with shoulder-length hair.) He is sitting calmly while looking at something off to his left.

Beneath his finery, Thomas was wearing his hair shirt. Of course, Holbein did not know that. Few people did, including the members of his family. William Roper told a story of one hot summer evening at supper, when Thomas was wearing a plain shirt without a collar, Anne Cresacre, his ward, noticed the edge of the hair shirt and laughed at it. Meg quickly signaled to her father and he, embarrassed, hastily covered it. Meg knew about it because she was the one who laundered it. Even Alice didn't learn about the hair shirt until long after they were married. She consulted Thomas's confessor and asked him to dissuade her husband, wondering how he washed it. That's when she learned that Meg was doing it. Apparently, though, they were the only family members who knew about it.

But let's return to the Holbein portrait. Thomas's father, John More, who would have been seventy-six years old at the time, is sitting to Thomas's right, dressed in a red robe and, like Thomas, head covered. He is gazing off into the distance. Lady Alice More is kneeling on a prie-dieu at the extreme right of the painting, her face serene and her eyes focused on an open book, probably a prayer book. (Holbein added a note on the sketch that said, "This one shall sit.") The other family members, left to right in the painting, are Elizabeth, who would have been twenty-one, with a book under her arm; adopted daughter Margaret Giggs, then twenty-two, seemingly pointing out something in a book to John More, who seems to be ignoring her; Thomas's ward

Ann Cresacre, then fifteen; Thomas's son John, then eighteen, looking at an open book; Cecily, then twenty, and Margaret, twenty-two, who are both kneeling, and it appears that Cecily might be holding a rosary.

There are two other people in the painting. One, peering out of a door in the background, is John Harris, Thomas's secretary. He wrote letters at Thomas's dictation and generally assisted him in his work. It was also he who usually read passages of Scripture during meals.

The Family "Fool"

The other person in the painting is Henry Patenson, known as the family "fool." He is standing beside Thomas's son John and is dressed fashionably in cap and robe. The role of a household fool dates from the twelfth century, but the idea of maintaining someone with diminished intelligence for the amusement of a family, as was so often done in medieval times, offends our sensibilities. There is, however, no indication anywhere that Henry Patenson was used as an object of amusement. He is said to have become crazed after a fall from a church steeple and Thomas kept him as a permanent member of his family, both out of pity for Henry and as a way to teach his children to care for those who weren't as gifted as they were.

The English fiction writer Anne Manning, who died in 1885, is not well-known today, but she wrote a fictional piece called *The Household of Sir Thomas More*. She included an account of the first meeting between Thomas and Henry Patenson. She wrote it as though it was a diary entry by Meg in October of 1524 when they would have still been living in Bucklersbury. If it didn't actually happen as she describes it, it should have. She wrote that, as she was walking with her father down a lane, they were accosted by a shabby fellow who quickly told them that he had once been a "smart chap" but then "fell from the church steeple and shook my brain-pan, I think, for its contents have seemed addled since. So what I want now is to be made a fool."

Manning's story continues:

"Then you are not one already?" says Father.

"If I were," says Patenson, "I should not have come to you."

"Why, like cleaves to like, you know they say," says Father.

"Aye," says the other, "but I've reason and feeling enough, too, to know you are no fool, though I thought you might want one. Great people like them at their tables, I've heard say, though I am sure I can't guess why, for it makes me sad to see fools laughed at; nevertheless, as I get laughed at already, I think I may as well get paid for the job if I can, being unable, now, to do a stroke of work in hot weather. And I'm the only son of my mother, and she is a widow. But perhaps I'm not bad enough."

"I know not that, poor knave," says Father, touched with quick pity, "and, for those that laugh at fools, my opinion, Patenson, is that they are the greater fools who laugh. To tell you the truth, I had had no mind to take a fool into my establishment, having always had a fancy to be prime fooler in it myself; however, you incline me to change my purpose, for as I said, like cleaves to like, so, I'll tell you what we will do—divide the business and go halves—I continuing the fooling, and you receiving the salary; that is, if I find, on inquiry, you are given to no vice, including that of scurrility."

"May it like your goodness," says poor Patenson, "I've been the subject, often, of scurrility, and affect it too little to offend that way myself. I ever keep

a civil tongue in my head, especially among young
ladies...."

"Meg, there is sense in this poor fellow," says father. "We will have him home and be kind to him."

And, sure enough, we have done so and been so
ever since.

Thomas sometimes took Henry with him on his travels.
One such time was Thomas's diplomatic mission to Bruges and
Calais in 1521. In Bruges it became apparent to some of the children that, as Thomas put it in writing about the episode, Henry
was a "man of special wit by himself and unlike the common
sort," and they began to throw stones at him. Henry gathered up
the stones and then stood on a bench, telling everyone to leave
the scene except those who threw the stones at him because he
planned to throw the stones back at them. Of course, he had
spoken in English and no one in Bruges understood what he
was saying, so they just laughed at him and continued to throw
the stones. So he threw stones back and, unfortunately, hit an
apparently innocent bystander in the head. Henry went up to
the man and told him, again in English, of course, to bear his
injuries bravely because he had been given fair warning.

There is one other figure in the painting, already mentioned—the family monkey. It seems to be clambering up Lady
Alice's dress, but she appears to be so accustomed to it that she
doesn't pay any attention to it. Apparently Holbein included
the monkey to indicate to those who would view the painting
that Thomas kept a large menagerie of animals. And indeed
he did. Among his "pets" were a fox, a weasel, a ferret, rabbits,
many breeds of birds, and, of course, that monkey. He had at
least some of those pets in Bucklersbury, too, because Erasmus
wrote about how Thomas loved to observe the animals' behavior, and it is assumed that those observations were responsible
for his remark that newly hatched chickens follow the nearest
human being.

Erasmus, too, apparently observed the behavior of animals while he visited Thomas. He wrote about the actions of a monkey and a weasel, explicitly setting the scene in Thomas's home: A monkey became ill, so was taken off its chain for a while. It watched a weasel trying to seize rabbits that were in their cages. When the weasel finally managed to pry loose the hutch so it was open at the back, the monkey quickly ran over to it, climbed on a plank, and restored the cage to its former safe position.

OTHER MEMBERS OF THE FAMILY

There are some family members, though, who are not in the Holbein painting—Thomas's three sons-in-law, his stepson-in-law, the husband of his adopted daughter, and grandchildren. By the time the painting was done in 1527, all of his daughters, stepdaughter and adopted daughter were married. Only his son and his ward, Anne, were still single; later they would marry each other. Margaret (Meg) married William Roper in 1521, and Cecily and Elizabeth married in a double wedding in 1525, Cecily to Giles Heron (who also had been Thomas's ward) and Elizabeth to William Dauncey. Alice's daughter, who is not in the painting, married Thomas Elrington, a wealthy landowner, in 1516. After Elrington died in 1523, Alice married Sir Giles Alington, another landowner. As already mentioned, Margaret Giggs, his adopted daughter, married John Clement, a doctor.

William Roper was a distinguished lawyer, from a long line of distinguished lawyers. His grandfather was Sir John Fineux, who was Chief Justice of the King's Bench until 1525. William's father, John, worked closely with Thomas's father while Thomas still had a private law practice. William succeeded his father as clerk of the pleas of the King's Bench, a position that he, in turn, later turned over to his son, Thomas's grandson.

Giles Heron's father had been the king's "treasurer of the

chamber," and William Dauncey's father had been a surveyor and then a member of the king's treasury. After his marriage to Elizabeth More, Dauncey was granted two leases within the Duchy of Cornwall, under Thomas's direct control, and in 1528 he became one of the tellers of the Exchequer. It's hard to imagine that Thomas wasn't responsible for his advancement.

Thomas's influence is even more easily seen in the fact that Roper, Heron and Dauncey were all three "elected" to Parliament in 1529. Heron and Dauncey both represented Thetford, which was part of the Duchy of Cornwall. It was the only time that Thetford was represented in the House of Commons. Roper was elected as a representative for Bramber in Sussex. Erasmus once said that no one became a member of the More household without attaining good fortune.

Good fortune, though, did not prevent illness. In 1529 Meg suffered from the sweating sickness that killed so many people in England at the time. Doctors had given up on her, and Thomas retreated to his private chapel and begged God to save her life. According to William Roper, Meg's husband, as Thomas prayed, "it came into his mind that an enema should be the only way to help her." He suggested it to the doctors, who wondered why they hadn't thought of it. After they administered it, Meg began to improve and eventually was restored to health.

The most famous visitor to Thomas's home in Chelsea, of course, was King Henry VIII. Roper wrote that the king liked Thomas's company so much that "suddenly sometimes he came home to his house at Chelsea to be merry with him." He wrote that, after dinner, the two walked in the gardens, the king "holding his arm around his neck."

Later, when Roper remarked to Thomas that he had never seen the king treat anyone else like that, Thomas replied, "I may tell you that I have no cause to be proud because of this; for if my head could win him a castle in France, it should not fail to go."

A Disastrous Fire

A famine inflicted England during 1528. That winter food was so scarce that Thomas and his family fed one hundred people a day. However, 1529 was different and there was a bountiful harvest, the first such in years. That fall the barns on the More farm were full when, suddenly, a fire broke out, apparently because of the negligence of a neighbor. It raged out of control for a while, destroying all of Thomas's barns, part of his home, and several of the neighbors' barns. This was seven weeks before Henry VIII appointed Thomas Lord Chancellor, but Thomas was in London attending the king when the fire broke out. Lady Alice sent Giles Heron to London to tell Thomas what had happened, and he stood by while Thomas wrote a letter back to Alice. After sympathizing with Alice, the letter said that God had permitted this to happen. Therefore:

> We must and are bound not only to be content but also to be glad. It was God who sent us all that we have lost and since he has by such a chance taken it away again, his pleasure be fulfilled. Let us heartily thank God as well for adversity as for prosperity, and perhaps we have more cause to thank him for our loss than for our gain, for his wisdom sees better what is good for us than we do ourselves.
>
> Therefore, I pray you be of good cheer and take all the household with you to church and there thank God both for what he has given us and for what he has taken from us and for what he has left us—which, if it pleases him, he can increase when he will; and if it pleases him to leave us yet less, so let it be as his pleasure.

He then instructed Alice to find out what their neighbors lost and to tell them that Thomas would make it up for them, because, he said, if any "poor neighbor of mine" would lose something because of what "happened in my house, I would not leave myself a spoon."

Since he didn't believe he could leave the king at that time and apparently was not even going home at night, Thomas told Alice to work out the best course of action to get the corn they would need for consumption in the winter and for planting in the spring. If it turned out that they had to sell some of the land to meet expenses, he told her not to discharge any of their workers without proper compensation or by finding them other employment. He ended the letter by saying that he would be home as soon as he could and sending good wishes to the children. He signed it, "Your loving husband."

CHAPTER 7

DEFENDER OF CATHOLICISM

In this chapter we present Thomas as a model for all those modern men and women, clerical and lay, who take it upon themselves to defend the Catholic Church against the anti-Catholicism that still exists today, not with his first effort (of which he was ashamed), but of succeeding books. The Church has not designated Thomas as one of the patrons of the Catholic Press, but he well could be. Much that he wrote in the sixteenth century applies just as well today.

Martin Luther had no idea of the consequences when he posted his ninety-five theses on the door of the church in Wittenberg, Germany on October 31, 1517. It was customary in academic circles to publicize a debate in this manner. Luther was angered by what he knew was a distortion of the Catholic doctrine of indulgences—the remission of temporal punishment for sins.

A Dominican friar named Johannes Tetzel was preaching that when a person dropped some money into the collection box to pay for an indulgence, the soul of his relative or friend at that instant sprang from purgatory into heaven. Tetzel was working for Archbishop Margrave Albrecht of Mainz and Magdeburg, who originally had the idea of preaching to the people a special indulgence whereby they could free the souls of dead relatives and friends from purgatory by paying money. The money was supposed to go to Rome to help finance the rebuilding of Saint Peter's Basilica.

However, Luther did more than post his theses on the door of the church. He also sent them to the German bishops, including Archbishop Albrecht. In a note to Albrecht, Luther wrote, "It [the preaching about the indulgence] has gone abroad in your name, but doubtless without your knowledge.... If agreeable to your grace, perhaps you would glance at my enclosed theses."

Albrecht, though, was furious because Luther had just shot down his money-raising project, so he complained to Rome. Pope Leo X, rather than consider the possibility of paying attention to Luther's criticisms, instructed the general of the Augustinians (the religious order to which Luther belonged) to silence him. By this time, though, others in Germany were taking up Luther's complaints. In 1519 he acknowledged that he no longer accepted the authority of the pope.

Erasmus learned quickly about Luther's theses and in the spring of 1518 he sent a copy of them to Thomas. At about the same time Luther wrote to a friend asking to obtain a copy of *Utopia*, so the two men were already aware of one another, although neither knew that in a few years they would be at each other's throats.

Once he started his call for reformation of the Church, Luther apparently couldn't stop. In 1520 he issued three pamphlets, their wide distribution aided by the invention of the printing press. *An Appeal to the Christian Nobility of the German Nation* urged the secular authorities to lead their communities away from Rome. In *Concerning the Babylonish Captivity of the Church*, he rejected all the sacraments except baptism and Communion, and in Communion he rejected the doctrine of transubstantiation as absurd. Finally, in *On the Liberty of a Christian Man*, Luther expounded his belief that salvation came from faith alone, without good works.

Up to that time, Erasmus had looked on Luther as a possible ally in his own efforts to reform the Church. But the attack on the Church's authority and its sacramental system was too much for Erasmus to consider Luther as a humanist reformer. Of course, it was too much for Pope Leo X, too. He issued a bull condemning Luther on forty-one counts and threatened to excommunicate him. Luther's response was to burn the papal document together with some books of canon law. So in January of 1521, Pope Leo solemnly excommunicated Luther.

In England, King Henry VIII took a central role in combating Luther. After Luther's second pamphlet was published, Henry wrote a *Defense of the Seven Sacraments*. He probably was helped by Edward Lee, Archbishop of York, and John Fisher, Bishop of Rochester. At some point the papers were given to Thomas, who offered some comments of his own and who put the book in order for printing. On May 12, 1521, Cardinal Wolsey led a procession to the churchyard of Saint Paul's Cathedral where he burned Luther's books while holding the king's manuscript. When the finished book was presented to Pope Leo in October, he rewarded Henry with the title "Defender of the Faith." (It was one of his last public acts because he died on December 1, 1521.)

THOMAS'S *RESPONSE TO LUTHER*

Luther responded in 1522 with *Against Henry, King of the English*. It was a vicious attack on Henry, calling him (among other things) a pig, dolt and liar who should be covered in excrement. He used much cruder and scatological language than I wish to repeat. When this reached England, Henry felt that, as king, he couldn't answer Luther in kind, so he gave Thomas the task of replying on his behalf in the same venomous language that Luther had used. It was not a task that Thomas wanted and he tried to have it published under a pseudonym, Guilielmus Rosseus (or William Ross), so people wouldn't know that Thomas was using the language present in the document.

An eighteenth-century minister, Francis Atterbury, was to call the finished product "the greatest heap of nasty language that perhaps was ever put together," the author of which had "the best knack of any man in Europe at calling bad names in good Latin." It is always described as polemic, an aggressive attack or refutation of the opinions or principles of another. His strongest polemic was against Luther for breaking his religious vows and marrying a former nun.

In *Responsio ad Lutherum* (*Response to Luther*), Thomas explained why he used scatological language. He said that he had been ordered to "clean out the dungy writings of Luther like the Augean stable," so he had to be willing to throw around what the animals left. Besides, some people read what Luther wrote only because of its vile language, so Thomas thought he could reach those people only by answering in kind.

He didn't publish his response immediately, however. He began it in February of 1523 and finished a first draft in about six weeks, but he didn't finish it until near the end of that year. The original title of the response ran like this (in Latin, of course): "The choice, learned, witty, pious work of the most learned William Ross in which he very admirably exposes and refutes the frantic calumnies with which the most foul buffoon, Luther, attacks the invincible king of England and France, Henry, the eighth by that name, the defender of the faith, renowned no less for his learning than for his royal power."

Between the first draft and the final product he discussed it with others and, in the process, clarified his own opinions on the nature of the Church and the role of the papacy. In fact, he changed his mind because he once believed that the papacy had been invented by men for political reasons rather than instituted by Christ. After study and discussion with his Italian friend Antonio Bonvisi, he admitted that he was wrong.

The completed response is both a defense of Henry VIII's document on the seven sacraments and an attack on Luther for rejecting the teachings of the Church. Thomas invoked the authority of the apostles and the early Church Fathers as well as the revelations of God or the teachings of the Holy Spirit. He saw the Church as the common corps of Christendom composed of "the common, known, Catholic people, clergy, lay folk and all, whatever their language is" and he said that they "stand together and agree in confession of the one true Catholic faith." He believed in the consensus of all those members of the Church much as he, as a lawyer, believed in the consensus of the people of England in the laws of the land.

Thomas saw the enemies of the Church to be the infidels and the heretics. The infidels were those outside the corporate body of the Church (mainly the Ottoman Turks, or Muslims, at that time). Luther clearly fell in the category of heretic, like those condemned by the councils of the Church. As one who had studied Saint Augustine's *City of God* years before, he continually paraphrased his maxim that "he would not have believed the gospel were it not for the authority of the Church."

His changed attitude toward the papacy, after his discussions with Bonvisi and his own studies, is shown in the long addition he made to his first draft. He wrote that the Christian faith was "what has been believed everywhere, always, and by all" (quoting Vincent of Lerins) and it was the duty of the pope, as Christ's representative on earth, to preserve and uphold that faith.

Luther was rejecting all authority, except his own, Thomas wrote, and thus was rejecting the teachings of all the Church Fathers and all believers of the past fifteen hundred years. He repeated several times Christ's promise that the gates of hell would not prevail against his Church. By what authority, he asked, could Luther establish his claims? Christ performed miracles to prove his authority, he said; what miracles had Luther performed? Why should any reasonable person believe him?

Thomas's lawyerly instincts were aroused when Luther claimed that "neither pope, nor bishop, nor any individual has the right to impose a single syllable on a Christian person, unless this is done by the latter's consent." To which Thomas replied, "Happy, therefore, are thieves and murderers, who will never be so insane as to agree to a law according to which they will pay penalties."

Luther's position that any Christian with faith "cannot lose his salvation by any sins, however great" also offended Thomas's sense of order. Such teaching, he wrote, seemed to "invite the whole world to security in sinning" and would "add spurs to those who rush toward all the worst actions."

Even while Thomas was responding to Luther, his own son-in-law, William Roper, began to expound Lutheran teachings. It got so notorious that Cardinal Wolsey summoned him to appear before him. Undoubtedly because of his connection to Thomas, Wolsey gave him only a "friendly warning" not to espouse his views in public, but Roper remained in heresy. Thomas had long discussions with him, but finally told Meg, "I have borne a long time with your husband; I have reasoned and argued with him on those points of religion, and still given to him my poor fatherly counsel, but I perceive that none of this is able to call him home." Therefore, he told his daughter, he would no longer argue and dispute with him, but "will clean give him over, and get me for a while to God and pray for him." Shortly after that, Roper returned to Catholicism, more fervent than before.

William Tyndale's English New Testament

As is obvious by the fact that Roper was enticed into Lutheranism for a time, Martin Luther's ideas spread quickly to England despite King Henry's and Thomas's documents. Luther, of course, was writing in German or Latin. But William Tyndale was writing in English. Tyndale was born in Gloucestershire, England. At Cambridge University, he became an admirer of Erasmus, translating his book *Enchiridion Militis Christiani* (*Manual of the Militant Christian*) into English. It included some of Erasmus's attacks on superstitious practices and some of the ceremonies of the Catholic Church. But Tyndale went much farther than Erasmus in his condemnation of these practices. At this time, the Church and the state in England were as one, and both ecclesiastical authorities and the civic leaders made life so hard for Tyndale that he left England and moved to the continent.

Tyndale translated the New Testament from Greek into English. Merchants in the Low Countries were glad to back him financially because they could see the large market for a Bible in English. In 1525, he began the printing in Cologne and completed it in Worms in 1526. It owed much to both Erasmus's Latin translation and Luther's German translation, but Tyndale wasn't satisfied with just a translation. In his commentary on Saint Paul's Letter to the Romans, for example, he affirmed Luther's doctrine of grace and redemption on faith alone.

The clergy in England were quick to condemn Tyndale's English New Testament and it was banned from the country. But the demand for it was enormous and merchants quickly found ways to smuggle it into the country. Many people thought they had received confirmation of what they had long been convinced—the clergy were withholding what the Bible truly taught in order to maintain their hold on the laity. Tyndale's New Testament was burned whenever authorities discovered it. Bishops' agents searched for concealed copies, bought consignments themselves, organized bonfires and took those who had copies to court.

Church authorities on the continent conducted a search for Tyndale, but he continued to elude them as he traveled from Cologne to Worms, Wittenberg, Antwerp and other places. He also composed two significant works, first *Parable of the Wicked Mammon* and then *The Obedience of a Christian Man*. He expounded Lutheran doctrines, especially the belief in justification through faith alone and his conviction that a temporal ruler should also exercise ecclesiastical power. In the second treatise he urged secular princes to rise up and reform the Church, as had been done in Germany. "The king is… without law… and shall give account to God alone," he wrote. It was something that Henry would take advantage of later—but not yet. He also taught that we are all priests of Christ and need have no other priest telling us what to do.

Soon numerous other books against the Catholic Church, in English, were making their way to England. Heresy was no longer underground. It was being debated at Oxford and Cambridge as well as among Catholics in the churches. Thomas became alarmed at the great harm this was doing to both the Church and society. He could see the collapse of the entire structure of the world as the heretics of Germany and Switzerland were trying to destroy the established order at the same time as the Muslim Turks were invading Western Europe. He explained to Erasmus:

> I am keenly aware of the risk involved in an open-door policy toward these newfangled, erroneous sects. Some people like to give an approving eye to novel ideas, out of superficial curiosity, and to dangerous ideas, out of devilry; and in so doing they assent to what they read, not because they believe it is true, but because they want it to be true.

THOMAS'S *A DIALOGUE CONCERNING HERESIES*

London's bishop, Cuthbert Tunstall, shared Thomas's fears. Finally, in 1528, Tunstall drew up a list of undesirable books and received permission from King Henry to have them banned. The list reached more than a hundred titles by 1529. Then he gave Thomas permission to read them in order to refute them—in English, of course. It would be the first major work of Thomas composed in English, although there was an English version of his *History of Richard III*. He had composed some poems in English, but that's about all. Except for the great English poet Geoffrey Chaucer, who died in 1400, most scholars and authors were still writing in Latin.

So Thomas published his first defense of Catholicism in English in 1529. He titled it *A Dialogue of Sir Thomas More* but it has come down to us as *A Dialogue Concerning Heresies*. Actually, the full title (in the early days of printing, long titles were common) was "A dialogue of Sir Thomas More, knight: one of the council of our sovereign lord the king and chancellor of his duchy of Lancaster. Wherein is treated divers matters as of the veneration and worship of images and relics, praying to saints, and going on pilgrimage. With many other things touching the pestilent sect of Luther and Tyndale by the one begun in Germany and by the other labored to be brought into England."

Almost five hundred years later, C.S. Lewis, while writing about Platonic dialogue in his masterpiece *English Literature in the Sixteenth Century, Excluding Drama*, called Thomas's book "perhaps the best specimen ever produced in English."

The dialogue consists of six conversations, over a period of time, which supposedly took place at Thomas's home in Chelsea. The conversations were between Thomas and a university student, called "the Messenger" in the book because he was sent by a friend of Thomas's to seek counsel concerning the new ideas he had been hearing about. Thomas showed great hospitality toward the young man, even though he arrived at seven o'clock in the morning. They interrupted their conversations four times for meals.

Thomas characterized the young man as highly articulate and witty, undoubtedly one of the reasons C.S. Lewis praised the book so highly. The first conversation consisted mainly of the young man's questions and concerns: devotional practices such as pilgrimages and praying to saints, but also about the harsh way the Church treated heretics, relying on law and public burnings. In this way, he said, "they act contrary to the mildness and merciful mind of Christ their master and against the example of all the old holy Fathers."

Thomas put off answering the young man's concerns. Feigning "lack of leisure," he asked him to return the following day. By that time he had mapped out a plan to address the issues raised. The conversations the second day began just before seven o'clock in Thomas's study. The two talked during the morning, broke for dinner, and then continued in the afternoon in the garden. The next conversations took place two weeks later, after the young man had time to discuss the issues with his friends. Again they talked all morning and all afternoon, the young man staying for both dinner and supper. Then they met one more time the next day, talking through the morning and ending with dinner together.

The conversation on the second day began with a discussion about truth: How do we know what is true? It's too simple, Thomas maintained, simply to deny the existence of miracles or to accept Luther's principle of Scripture only. At one point Thomas asked the "Messenger" if someone should "better trust his eyes than his wit." The young man replied that he thought his eyes were quite reliable. But Thomas replied that the eyes might be deceived, as in the case of a magician (he calls him a juggler) who cuts something up before your face and then makes it whole again, or "puts a knife into his eye and sees never the worse."

Thomas showed himself a master at keeping the reader's attention, mixing humor with the more serious parts of the conversation. Some of his best "merry" tales, as he referred to them, are in this dialogue. But returning to the subject, he told the young man that, just as we learn from experience that our eyes do not perceive everything accurately, so we must realize that one cannot read and interpret everything, including Scripture, only by one's own wit. In order to read Scripture according to the mind of its author, he said, one must have a well-trained reason and access to the vast collective learning of the Catholic Church.

In the garden during the afternoon, the two men discussed the nature and necessity of the Catholic Church. Thomas saw the Church as a visible Church, founded by Christ and with a tradition and hierarchy stretching back for fifteen hundred years. It had been guided by the Holy Spirit since his descent on the apostles at Pentecost. Its teachings were transmitted, both through Scripture and orally, by the Church Fathers—to teach what Jesus taught. Only after establishing that did Thomas bring the dialogue back to such things as pilgrimages, the veneration of images and relics, and saints. He said that the divine origin of the Church was proved by miracles and reinforced by pilgrimages. At the end of the day, the "Messenger" said that he felt satisfied, but Thomas set up another time to discuss other issues.

Sure enough, after a couple weeks, the young man had other questions that rose from discussions he had had with his university friends. The main problem they saw was the Church's efforts to keep Tyndale's translation of the New Testament away from the people. They saw this as the clergy's attempt to keep the laity under their control and to keep them from reading about clerical abuses. Thomas, though, insisted that the problem was Tyndale's Lutheran interpretations. Thomas said that he, too, would like to see an English translation, but only one that was faithful to the Greek text and is approved by the Church.

Tyndale and Luther, Thomas said, went far beyond a desire to make Scripture available to the ordinary Catholic. They denied the Church's authority and the validity of all the sacraments except baptism and Communion. They also denied that humans have free will and thus put the responsibility for evil on God. And, especially, they preached that their doctrine of liberty meant that one who has faith needs nothing else. Thomas saw Luther's call for personal freedom that is independent of "all governors and all laws, spiritual or temporal, except the Gospel" as paving the way for war.

In fact, war had already broken out in Germany when the peasants revolted in 1525. Thomas also blamed Luther for the sacking of Rome in 1527 (the forces of Emperor Charles V included German Lutheran soldiers). Thomas reported on the sacking in horrifying detail, from reports he had received from diplomats, to show what happens when people are encouraged to disrespect the law.

Thomas thought that Luther's denial of free will was "the very worst and most mischievous heresy that ever was thought upon, and also the most mad." The young man seemed to accept that, but asked why the Church and the state treated the heretics so cruelly. Why not just convince reasonable people how foolish the heretical teachings were rather than arresting them and, in some cases, burning them at the stake?

Thomas's answer was that the state occasionally has to step in because Luther stirred many people to angry violence against institutions protected by the law. Force is sometimes necessary, he said, to preserve peace and justice. He called on history to show that it was the "reformers" who first used violence, driving "good princes" to use force for the "preservation not only of the faith but also of the peace among their people."

With his knowledge of the Church Fathers, Thomas was able to show that even Saints Augustine and Jerome approved of physical force, but not by the Church. He said that Saint Augustine had argued against the Donatists for much of his life and "had with great patience borne and suffered their malice, only writing and preaching in reproof of their errors, and had not only done them no temporal harm, but also had prevented and resisted others who would have done it." Eventually, though, Augustine had to have recourse to the government and to exhort "Count Boniface and others to repress them with force and threaten them with bodily punishment."

Thomas pointed out that the Church Fathers didn't allow the Church to use physical force, but only the civil government. He thought that the ruler had a civil and moral obligation to use such force to safeguard his people and to "defend his good and harmless neighbor against the malice and cruelty of the wrongdoer."

Thomas then gave the "Messenger" several passages to read, one from the Church's official book of Church law and others from Saints Augustine and Cyprian. He also gave him some passages from Luther's and Tyndale's books and asked him to compare what they said with the teachings of the Church Fathers. The young man took them with him and read them overnight, returning the next morning to announce that he was now convinced because Tyndale and Luther are "so plainly confuted by the old holy Fathers." If he had seen so much before, he said, "it would probably have shortened much of our long communication."

Thomas replied that it was possible that Luther and Tyndale would gain many followers and, perhaps, the number of true Christians could be reduced to a small sect. However, he said, whatever might happen in the near future, Christ's Church would grow large again. Then, as the two men sat down for a final meal together, Thomas prayed that all might be one flock again, "filled with charity in the way of good works in this wretched world that we may be partners of the heavenly bliss which the blood of God's own Son has bought us."

Thomas's brother-in-law, John Rastell, published *Dialogue Concerning Heresies* in 1529. Two years later Thomas's nephew, William Rastell, published a second edition for which Thomas added some pages about the dangers of heretical books. By then, of course, he was Lord Chancellor.

Thomas's *The Supplication of Souls*

However, while he was still writing the first edition of the book, a man by the name of Simon Fish, an Englishman who had wisely moved to Antwerp, wrote a violently anti-clerical pamphlet titled *Supplication for the Beggars*. He accused the English clergy of impoverishing the country by grabbing as much land and titles as they could, a full third of the property in the kingdom. Furthermore, he accused the clergy of debauching one hundred thousand women! He suggested to King Henry that he assert his power over the clergy, intimating that he should appropriate church properties. He wrote that the practice of saying Masses for the dead was just one more way for priests to wrest money from the people.

As soon as Thomas read the pamphlet, he composed a reply almost ten times the length of Fish's seventeen-page pamphlet. He called his response *The Supplication of Souls*, warning his readers of those who were working not only to destroy the clergy "by whom we are much helped," but also to spread the poisonous opinion that purgatory did not exist. Those souls in purgatory, he wrote, were calling for prayers and remembrance "in most piteous ways." Thomas apparently thought of purgatory as most of his contemporaries did, rather than as our Church today describes it as a state or process of purification. Hence Thomas wrote that the souls were crying out, "the gay clothes burning upon our backs and those proud pearled pastys (ornaments dangled from their hair) hang hot about our cheeks." He asked his readers if they wouldn't reach out to snatch their mother from the fire.

However, Thomas wrote, those souls in purgatory were warning that Simon Fish's main purpose was "to inflame the King's Highness against the Church." If he was successful in turning his "beggars" against "bishops, abbots, priors, prelates, and priests," Thomas wrote, he next would turn against the laity. He vehemently denied that the clergy were seizing the wealth of the kingdom and said that the seizure of church lands would be followed by the theft of other property, and the assault on the Church would lead to an attack on all forms of authority. What had occurred in Germany, he wrote, could happen in England as well. He was warning King Henry not to listen to the voices of the anti-clerics because they would "bring all the realm to ruin, and this not without butchery and foul bloody hands."

To counteract this, Thomas called for "good wholesome laws to help in all these matters." Perhaps Henry listened to Thomas because slightly more than a month later the king made Thomas his Lord Chancellor.

CHAPTER 8

ENGLAND'S LORD CHANCELLOR

Thomas is again a model for modern politicians who should perform their public duties to the best of their abilities despite the pressures that they might face. He is also a model for all Catholic lay men and women who recognize their obligation to occasionally take the lead in defending the Church in the public square. Unfortunately, in Thomas's case, he too often stood nearly alone in opposing the forces that would soon destroy the Church in England.

Why did King Henry VIII appoint Thomas Lord Chancellor? And why did Thomas accept the position?

Of course Henry had long valued Thomas's advice and followed it many times through the years. We have seen that he liked to visit the More home and to walk with Thomas in his garden while conversing with him. This was during the time when Henry was a devout Catholic, for which the pope named him "Defender of the Faith" for his defense against Martin Luther. He was exceptionally pious and even attended several Masses each day. He was a proficient linguist who wrote Latin with style, an excellent musician on the lute and organ, and a composer of songs. As a young man he was an excellent athlete who enjoyed jousting.

But Henry had changed and Thomas could not possibly have been unaware of it. He became obsessed with having a male heir, and his wife Catherine didn't provide him with one. Catherine, the youngest daughter of Ferdinand and Isabella of Spain, had first married Henry's brother Arthur in 1501. After Arthur's death, Henry received a dispensation from Pope Julius II to marry his sister-in-law in 1509. They had children, but only Mary survived. Sometime before 1526, Henry fell in love with Anne Boleyn after first having had a sexual affair with her sister.

During the summer of 1526, his love for Anne combined with a religious scruple and Henry began to doubt the validity of his marriage to Catherine. He had married his dead brother's wife against the injunctions of the Old Testament Book of Leviticus. The verses he found in that book were 18:16, which says, "You shall not have intercourse with your brother's wife, for that would be a disgrace to your brother," and 20:21, which says, "If a man marries his brother's wife and thus disgraces his brother, they shall be childless because of this incest."

He was determined to have his marriage to Catherine annulled so he could marry Anne. In 1527 he asked Cardinal Wolsey to expedite the matter secretly. A Church court, though, came to no conclusion and Henry decided to appeal to Pope Clement VII, asking him to declare that the marriage was invalid. It was not a propitious time for the pope, who was a virtual prisoner of Emperor Charles, Catherine's nephew, after the sacking of Rome in 1527. However, in 1528 the pope dispatched Cardinal Lorenzo Campeggio to England with instructions for him and Cardinal Wolsey to study the matter. It wasn't until May of 1529, though, that Cardinal Campeggio convened a legatine court (one conducted by a legate) in the Parliament chamber of Blackfriars to hear the case.

All this, of course, was prior to Thomas's appointment as Lord Chancellor. As advisor to both King Henry and Cardinal Wolsey, though, he knew what was going on. His sympathies were with Queen Catherine, whom he admired, but he kept his opinions to himself.

HENRY EXPLAINS THE CASE TO THOMAS

The first time the king spoke with Thomas about the matter seems to have been in September of 1527 after Thomas's return from France where he and Cardinal Wolsey ratified that year's treaty with King Francis I. As Thomas later wrote, he was with Henry at Hampton Court, where the king was staying, when "suddenly his Highness walking in the gallery, broke with me of his great matter." He said that Henry declared that his marriage to Catherine had been contrary to the laws of the Church, of God and of nature itself. The king then "laid the Bible open before me, and there read me the words that moved his Highness and diverse other erudite persons so to think, and asked me further what I thought about it."

Thomas's answer was noncommittal, saying that he distrusted his "poor mind." That answer, naturally, didn't satisfy the king, who ordered him to talk to certain royal advisors about the matter and to read a book on the need for an annulment.

Thomas was determined to stay out of what came to be known as the king's "great matter," the issue that was to dominate the course of action in the kingdom for the next five years. Thomas said later that he never "meddled" in the affair because he considered the matter to be in the hands of an ordinary process of Church law. He obviously thought it prudent to stay out of it, but also to accept whatever the Church ruled on the matter.

He certainly thought about it, though. William Roper reported a conversation he had with his father-in-law about this time. Thomas said that he had three wishes: that there would be peace among the Christian nations then fighting one another, that the many heresies then present would be settled in "a perfect uniformity of religion," and that the king's matter of his marriage would "to the glory of God and quietness of all parts be brought to a good conclusion."

Two days before the legatine court formally opened on May

31, 1529, Catherine met with the Archbishop of Canterbury and eight other bishops to declare before them that she wanted the matter revoked to Rome. Bishop John Fisher of Rochester was Catherine's counsel and supporter. When the court itself opened at Blackfriars, she delivered a formal protest against the process to which she was being subjected. She was asked to return the following Monday.

On that day, when she was asked to come forth, she rose from her seat and walked over to the king. She knelt at his feet and asked, "Wherein have I offended you?" She went on to say that she loved all those whom he loved only for his sake. He lifted her up and said that it was only because of his love for her that he never mentioned his doubts about the validity of the marriage. Furthermore, he said, if the court ruled that their marriage was valid, he would gladly be reunited with her. With that, she left the court.

Thomas undoubtedly was among the many people who attended that hearing, but he was not there for the rest of the session. The court didn't adjourn for a month, but Thomas had to leave for France again to negotiate the Peace of Cambrai. Cardinal Wolsey obviously couldn't attend the negotiation since the king's "great matter" was his primary responsibility, so Thomas and Bishop Tunstall were England's delegates. (See Chapter 5.)

As we said at the end of Chapter 5, Thomas found everything changed when he returned to England. Wolsey had failed to obtain the annulment for Henry, was indicted and arrested for treason, and surrendered the Great Seal that indicated his office as Lord Chancellor. He was permitted to continue as Archbishop of York, but a year later he was summoned to London to face his charges. He died at Leicester Abbey on his way there.

WHY HENRY APPOINTED THOMAS LORD CHANCELLOR

On October 25, 1529, King Henry VIII appointed Thomas Lord Chancellor, and gave him the Great Seal. So we repeat the questions we posed at the beginning of this chapter: Why did King Henry VIII appoint Thomas Lord Chancellor? And why did Thomas accept the position?

Henry certainly knew Thomas's opinion about his "great matter," even if they had discussed it only that one time. He could have appointed William Warham, the Archbishop of Canterbury, or Cuthbert Tunstall, the Bishop of London. After all, no layman had been Lord Chancellor for almost a hundred years; the position usually went to an archbishop, so close the Church and the state had been. However, it probably was precisely because Thomas was a layman that Henry appointed him—to assert his power over that of the Church.

Other than the issue of the king's "great matter," and if the king wanted a layman in that position, Thomas was the logical person. No one else in England could rival his reputation as a skilled lawyer, judge, diplomat and statesman. His fame as a humanist scholar and author gave him even more authority. He had been an outstanding success as Speaker of the House of Commons, Chancellor of the Duchy of Lancaster, and as a representative of England in foreign negotiations. But beyond all that, he had worked closely with Henry for more than ten years and Henry was confident of his loyalty and good judgment. Even the fact that Thomas was known to support Queen Catherine might have influenced Henry in his decision because he knew that Catherine was popular among the people and it didn't hurt to have Thomas at his side.

And why did Thomas accept the position? First of all, it should be obvious that few politicians would refuse to accept the second highest position in all of England. It was the culmination of his professional life, and it certainly pleased his wife and, especially, his father, who was already ailing. However, Thomas probably looked on it as the will of God. He had never sought an office but had always performed his duties in whatever office was given to him, and the Chancellorship was no exception. He was undoubtedly truthful when he wrote to Erasmus that he accepted the Chancellorship because of his concern for the affairs of Christendom. He thought that it was God's will for him to be in that position where he could best defend the Church against the heretics who were threatening it. He called it his "bounden duty." Perhaps he also thought that he could protect the Church against the wrath of the king.

Shortly after his appointment, Henry again approached Thomas about his "great matter." As Thomas wrote later, the king asked him to ponder the question of his annulment and, if persuaded, "would gladly use me among other of his counselors." The king asked others to try to persuade Thomas. Thomas listened attentively to the various arguments, but was convinced that the original papal dispensation that permitted Henry to marry the wife of his deceased brother was valid, and hence the marriage was also valid. Naturally, Henry was disappointed but, according to Thomas, "nevertheless gracious lord."

THOMAS EMBODIED THE LAW IN ENGLAND

The position of Lord Chancellor was not quite the same as today's prime minister because the king was much more powerful than the king or queen of England is today. However, once installed as Lord Chancellor, Thomas was a busy man indeed. The king called Parliament into session in November and Thomas spearheaded new laws that the king wanted passed. At the same time, he was engaged in all other affairs of state including foreign relations. In December, for example, while Parliament was still in session, he conducted negotiations with the Spanish ambassador on matters of trade.

But the Lord Chancellor performed some duties that are not the province of today's prime minister. For thirty-one months he embodied the law in England, presiding at both the

Courts of Chancery and the Star Chamber. Both dealt with civil actions, but the Star Chamber was concerned mainly with cases that involved criminality of some sort, while the Courts of Chancery settled disputes among the citizens of England.

Legal historian John Guy tells us that, in those courts, Thomas handled an average of nine hundred twelve cases per year, compared to five hundred thirty-five cases per year handled by Cardinal Wolsey when he was chancellor. Guy reviewed the archival records of the two thousand three hundred fifty-six suits that came before the courts during Thomas's thirty-one months in office. He said that Thomas "cultivated a distinctive policy of self-involvement, scrupulousness, and discretion." He said that Thomas's greatest contribution was "to rejuvenate the ancient theory that judges had a personal duty in conscience to see right done by all whose business was entertained in the courts they directed."

Thomas did indeed see his position as chief judge differently than had Cardinal Wolsey since Thomas had much more experience and legal knowledge. He said that he saw his role was to make his judgments "grounded upon the law of reason and the law of God." That meant that he sometimes corrected injustices that occurred in the ordinary courts.

At one point, he learned that some judges were complaining about his reversals of their decisions, so he called them together for a dinner in the council chamber at Westminster. After dinner he reviewed with them all the cases they were complaining about and convinced them that they would have made the same decisions if they were in Thomas's position. He then proposed that they also use their discretion to moderate the rigors of the law, but they refused his suggestion. He later told William Roper that the judges preferred not to make individual decisions when they could fall back on the verdict of a jury and the strict application of the law.

Thomas's reputation for fairness, already considerable, grew during his years as England's chief judge. That applied to his family as well. He was judge when his son-in-law, Giles

Heron, filed a suit in the Chancery, "presuming too much of his favor," as Roper wrote. In the court it's known as *Giles Heron v. Nicholas Millisante*, in bundle six hundred forty-three of the proceedings. Thomas heard the case without recusing himself as a modern judge would do, and, as Roper wrote, "made in conclusion a flat decree against him."

Cresacre More wrote another tale about Thomas's fairness that involved his family, this time his wife. The story might or might not have actually happened. A beggar-woman had lost her dog and it found its way to the More household, where Lady Alice adopted it. The beggar learned where the dog was and complained to Thomas. In order to make sure that the dog really belonged to the woman, he had her stand at one end of a hall and Alice at the other, with the dog in the middle. Then both women were told to call for the dog. It went to the beggar-woman, so Thomas returned it to her. Then, though, Alice bargained with the woman and bought the dog for a piece of gold. Cresacre More ends the anecdote, "So all parties were agreed; everyone smiling to see his manner of inquiring out the truth."

Administering Justice to Heretics

Part of the justice that Thomas administered was to heretics. He had been writing against their heresies and now he was in a position to do something more substantial. In a letter to Erasmus, he wrote that he was going to be as active as he could against the heretics because the future of the world itself was in peril. Heretical books still made their way to England, and Thomas tried to put a stop to it. He and Bishop John Stokesley, who succeeded Cuthbert Tunstall as Bishop of London after Tunstall was named Bishop of Durham, developed a network of spies who provided them with information, and they condoned some types of torture to ferret out information. Some of the interrogations took place in Thomas's home in Chelsea, although he vigorously denied using torture. He also personally led raids on the homes of merchants who, informants had reported, had smuggled heretical books into England.

He also approved of burning heretics at the stake, something that we today find incongruous with the idea of a saint. He believed in corporal punishment, including burning, and in this he was no different from most of his contemporaries. He wrote that heresy in England, "a good Catholic realm," had for centuries been punished by death in a fire, and there's no doubt that he was right. John A. Guy, in his book *Tudor England*, estimated that nearly thirty heretics had been burned in the century before Thomas's chancellorship. That would continue after Thomas's death, too, during the reign of Catholic Queen Mary, when Thomas Cranmer, the Archbishop of Canterbury, among others, would be burned.

It was unique, to put it mildly, for Thomas as a layman to take the lead in defending the Church. In the sixteenth century, as in most of Christian history, that was supposed to be the function of the clergy. But, of course, these were unique times as the Protestant Reformation was growing on the continent, especially in Germany and Switzerland. In England, Bishops John Fisher and John Stokesley were doing their best to combat heresy, but the leader was clearly a layman, Sir Thomas More. He was centuries ahead of the Church, which in 1965, in the Second Vatican Council's *Decree on the Apostolate of the Laity*, would tell lay people that it is their responsibility to renew the temporal order.

Members of the clergy recognized Thomas's leadership. In the spring of 1530, the Benedictine Foundation of Christ Church in Canterbury awarded Thomas and Alice a letter of confraternity. During that year, too, an ecclesiastical commission, with Thomas the only lay member, met at Westminster to discuss heretical literature. In June of that year, Thomas issued another proclamation against heretical books, banning all translations of the Bible into English since those translations always included heretical commentaries.

It was about this time, during the winter of 1530, that

Thomas's father died. He was in his late seventies. He was spared witnessing what was to happen to his son, and Thomas included on his own epitaph only that his father died "having witnessed his son made Lord Chancellor of England." According to William Roper, as his father was dying, Thomas "with tears taking him about the neck, most lovingly kissed and embraced him, commending him into the merciful hands of almighty God."

After his father's death, Thomas began to complain of some disease of the chest and he claimed that he felt himself growing old. He had many more troubles ahead though.

HENRY'S CAMPAIGN TO HAVE HIS MARRIAGE ANNULLED

While Thomas was busy fighting heretics, King Henry was trying to figure out how to get the Church to agree to the annulment of his marriage to Catherine. By this time, three factions had developed in the kingdom. The first was those who, like Thomas, supported Catherine, but it also included those nobles who feared that her nephew Emperor Charles V would wage war against England if Henry succeeded in having the marriage annulled. The second, led by Thomas Cranmer, Thomas Cromwell, the Boleyn family, and the legal scholar Christopher St. German, wanted Henry to destroy the Church's independent status and make it subordinate to the king. The third, led by Thomas Howard, the Duke of Norfolk, was happy with the status quo.

Cranmer's plan was to convince Parliament to declare Henry as head of both Church and state, and, as such, obtain his annulment. Cranmer worked throughout 1530 on a theological defense of Henry's caesaropapist power. He was able to get the support of Bishop Stokesley and Archbishop Edward Lee of York, who gathered supporting documents. They then went first to the faculties of the universities of Oxford and Cambridge, which eventually agreed with Cranmer that it was "more probable" that Henry should not have been permitted to marry his dead brother's wife if she had been "carnally known." Catherine claimed, however, to have been a virgin when she married Henry, and Thomas believed her.

In June of 1530 Henry called a meeting of lords and prelates to put their signature on a letter to Pope Clement VII, asking him to "declare by your authority what so many learned men proclaim," that is, that Henry's marriage to Catherine was invalid. Naturally, Thomas's name doesn't appear on that letter. He might have refused to sign it, but it's more probable that he wasn't asked to do so since his opinion was so widely known. He was by this time being excluded from anything having to do with the king's "great matter."

By September of 1530 Cranmer compiled what is known as the *Collectanea satis copiosa*, a collection of historical documents, ranging back from the Donation of Constantine to Geoffrey of Monmouth's *History of the Kings of Britain*. Its purpose was to show that Henry, as the ruler of an empire, had inherited the power of ecclesiastical as well as civil jurisdiction. The collection was presented to Henry, who read it with great relish. He seems to have been sincerely convinced that he was the rightful head of the Catholic Church in England.

He decided to use that authority. Later that month he explained his imperial rights to the papal nuncio and forbade the exercise of any papal authority in England. He issued a proclamation against any papal bulls detrimental to the king's concerns. That was too much for Thomas, and he expressed his disagreement. That angered Henry and he thought about dismissing him as Lord Chancellor, but didn't do so because there were still many nobles, lawyers and prelates who shared Thomas's views. However, the king began to complain that Thomas had not signed that letter to the pope and there were rumors that he might be forced to resign. But not yet.

Henry realized that he still needed the support of the clergy and Parliament. In October he convened a meeting of lawyers and members of the clergy and asked them if Parliament should enact a law that Henry's divorce should be decided by the Archbishop of Canterbury. The answer angered Henry because the advisors "deliberatively answered that it could not be done." He determined to try anyway.

At this point, two men came to Henry's rescue. Christopher St. German was a highly influential lawyer whose book *Doctor and Student* argued that English common law should have precedence over canon law. And Thomas Cromwell became Henry's chief advisor.

In January of 1531 Henry convened Parliament. As was customary, the Convocation of Clergy met at the same time. In an attempt to intimidate the clergy, Henry accused them of praemunire, an offense against the king, for having ecclesiastical courts, and he demanded that they recognize him as head of the Church in England. Bishop John Fisher was the leader of the bishops who opposed him. He said, "We cannot grant this to the king without abandoning our unity with the See of Rome… and so leap out of Peter's ship to be drowned in the waves of all heresies, sects, schisms and divisions."

In March Thomas performed what undoubtedly was a difficult task for him. On behalf of the king, he read a statement to the House of Lords about Henry's marriage. He told them that Henry had sought an annulment for reasons of conscience and religion, not out of love for some lady. Then, though, he was asked for his own opinion about the matter and, according to an account of the proceedings, replied simply that "he had many times already declared it to the king; and he said no more."

From the House of Lords Thomas proceeded to the House of Commons where he read a similar statement. According to William Roper, after these performances Thomas talked with the Duke of Norfolk about his wish to resign as Lord Chancellor. He knew that the king was using him, and he resented it. However, he did not resign.

THOMAS'S CONFUTATION OF TYNDALE'S ANSWER

That was the situation, in the spring of 1531, when William Tyndale published *An Answer unto Sir Thomas More's Dialogue*, a rebuttal of what we know as Thomas's *Dialogue Concerning Heresies*. He used it to mount an attack on the Catholic Church's teachings regarding the sacraments and he espoused again the Lutheran teachings against communal worship and ritual, for faith rather than works, and for everyone's right to interpret Scripture.

As soon as Thomas received Tyndale's book, he went into a frenzied period during which he worked far into the night, by candlelight, writing a refutation. He realized that Henry had been influenced by Tyndale's earlier book *The Obedience of a Christian Man* (it's believed that Anne Boleyn gave a copy to him) and Thomas now was convinced that the fate of England, and perhaps all of Christendom, was at stake. He was well aware that Cromwell, St. German and Cranmer (among others) were encouraging Henry in his determination to rule both the Church and the state. Through his writings, he hoped, he could indirectly appeal to the king's conscience while also defending the Catholic Church.

The result was the longest polemic writing, at least in English, in history—a half-million words, divided into eight books, three of which were published before Thomas resigned as Lord Chancellor. He called it *Confutation of Tyndale's Answer* and it, like most of Thomas's books, was in the form of a dialogue between Tyndale and himself, allowing him to answer Tyndale's charges point by point.

He also recalled the effective role Henry had played in the past, when he published his *Defense of the Seven Sacraments*. He said, in fact, that in writing this book, Thomas was only imitating the king and fulfilling the same duty they both had when they took their oaths of office—this is, to defend the independence of the Church.

He insisted that there was only one true Church, the one founded by Christ and that continued to exist as the Catholic Church. He acknowledged that, through history, some of its members had been weak, but that didn't affect its authority or the holiness of the Church. Tyndale, on the other hand, was preaching a vision of private belief and individual grace. Thomas distinguished between "an historical faith" and Tyndale's "feeling faith."

One of the things that spurred Thomas on, as week after week he wrote thousands of words, was his conviction that "the great arch-heretic Antichrist" was about to come. He thought of Tyndale and Luther as the Antichrist's false prophets or disciples. Therefore, he begged his readers not to read any heretical books, even, in one remarkable passage, his own books in case his very mention of heretical beliefs might contaminate them.

The eight volumes of *Confutation of Tyndale's Answer* have been criticized for being repetitive and too long, a point that even Thomas at one point acknowledged when he wrote, "My writing is over long, and therefore too tedious to read." His excuse for this was that he felt required to concentrate on certain key themes and doctrines so his readers "shall not need to read over any chapter but one."

The King Wins and Thomas Resigns

Thomas published the first three books of his *Confutation* in March of 1532, shortly after Parliament resumed its deliberations. Cromwell had used most of the previous year spreading discontent against the clergy and he now proposed the Restraint of Annates Act. "Annates" were taxes the clergy sent to Rome and Cromwell knew that they were unpopular among the laity. Another bill, the Supplication of the Commons Against the Ordinaries, reflected St. German's objections to clerical courts.

William Warham, the Archbishop of Canterbury, now in his eighties, was presiding over the Convocation of the Clergy, and he resisted. He prepared a powerful speech against the bill, but he died before he could give it.

That left only Bishop Fisher, among the bishops, with the courage to oppose the king, and he was seriously ill. Other fearless Religious included William Peto and Henry Elstow of the Franciscan Observants at Greenwich. Peto was particularly forceful, at Easter time preaching directly to the king, telling him, "Your Highness's preachers are too much like those of Ahab's days, in whose mouths was found a false and lying spirit. Theirs is the gospel of untruth."

If that wasn't forceful enough, Father Peto continued, "I beseech your Grace to take good heed, lest if you will need follow Ahab in his doings, you will surely incur his unhappy end also, and that the dogs lick your blood as they licked Ahab's—which God avert and forbid." Father Peto was soon arrested and confined within Lambeth Palace.

On May 13, Cromwell prepared a bill that would transfer the powers of the Church to Parliament. Included was a stipulation that the Church would not have the power to arrest people accused of heresy. This seemed to be the last straw from Thomas, who voiced his thorough opposition. By then, though, it was too late. On May 15, the Convocation of Clergy accepted the king's demands in a document known as the "submission of the clergy." From then on, all ecclesiastical law required the king's approval. He was truly the head of the Church in England.

On the next day, May 16, 1532, Thomas went to the garden at York Place, where the king was waiting with Thomas Howard, the Duke of Norfolk. Thomas had with him the pouch that contained the Great Seal of England, and he ceremonially handed it back to Henry. Thomas wrote later that the king received the pouch graciously and then granted him leave to spend the rest of his life in preparing his soul "in the service of God. And for the service which you before have done me, you will find me a good and gracious lord to you in any suit which should concern your honor or pertain to your profit."

Thomas bowed and withdrew. It would be the last time the two men would be together.

CHAPTER 9

RETIREMENT AT CHELSEA

Like some modern politicians, Thomas had resigned because he couldn't continue to support his king. Now he hoped for a peaceful retirement during which he could keep busy with his writing while enjoying his family. That, of course, was not to be. He had stuck to his principles but that no longer was sufficient for the king and those who sought his favor. Now all he could do was to try to protect his family as he worried about what was to come.

"Chancellor More is Chancellor no more." That's how the More family's "fool," Henry Patenson, spread the news that Thomas had resigned as Lord Chancellor of England.

After resigning, Thomas returned to Chelsea where he found his wife Alice in church. It was their custom, when they attended Mass together, to sit in different parts of the church since Thomas could serve at the Mass and Alice couldn't. After Mass, one of their attendants would go to Alice's pew and announce, "May it please your Ladyship to come forth now my Lord is gone." Therefore, after his resignation, Thomas approached Alice's pew with his cap in his hand and said, "May it please your Ladyship to come forth now my Lord is gone."

According to William Roper, Alice thought that Thomas was joking, as usual. She responded gruffly, "No doubt it pleases you, Master More, to joke in this way."

Thomas replied, "I speak seriously, and it is as I say: my Lord Chancellor is gone and is no longer here."

Roper wrote no more about the incident, but Thomas Stapleton wrote that, when Alice learned the whole story she was in great distress at her husband's loss of position.

So Thomas tried to retire to his home in Chelsea. The "official" reason given for his resignation, as he wrote in three letters during that period, was because of his poor health and it was said that the king accepted the resignation reluctantly. Some things never change. Thomas was concerned about his reputation and, a year after the resignation, he wrote to Erasmus about the way things stood at that time:

> So far no one has advanced a complaint against my integrity. Either my life has been so spotless or, at any rate, I have been so circumspect that if my rivals oppose my boasting of the one, they are forced to let me boast of the other. As a matter of fact, the king himself has pronounced on this situation at various times —frequently in private, and twice in public. It is embarrassing for me to relate, but on the occasion of the installation of my most distinguished successor, the king used as his mouthpiece the most illustrious duke—I mean the Duke of Norfolk, who is the Lord High Treasurer of England, and he respectfully ordered the duke to proclaim publicly that he had unwillingly yielded to my request for resignation. The king, however, was not satisfied even with that extraordinary manifestation of good will toward me; at a much later date, he had the same pronouncement repeated, in his presence, at a solemn session of the Lords and Commons, this time using my successor as his mouthpiece.

So for about a year, Thomas was allowed to retire in peace. He wasn't idle, though, because it was during that time that he completed books four through eight of his *Confutation of Tyndale's Answer,* which was eventually published in the spring of 1533. He also wrote his epitaph during that year, having it carved for the stone tomb where he hoped to be buried. He ended the epitaph by saying that he was relieved of the "business of this life" in order to prepare his soul for immortality. An interesting point about the epitaph is that it makes no mention of any of his writings, either *Utopia* and his other humanist writings or his polemic writings in defense of the Church.

As he retired to Chelsea, Thomas made a conscious effort to simplify his life, indeed, to live a secluded, almost monastic, life. In a letter to Erasmus, he said that his doctors had prescribed such a life, but he doubtless also wished to do it for spiritual reasons. Roper reported that he gathered his family around him and asked their advice on how they might continue to live as they had been, considering that his income was greatly reduced. Receiving no replies, he used one of his favorite phrases, "Then I will show my poor mind to you." He suggested that they should all now contribute to the cost of the household and that they should modify their "diet" in the future.

He was still far from impoverished because he continued to draw an income as a king's councilor until 1534, and he still owned estates in Oxfordshire, Herfordshire and Kent. Furthermore, Alice owned land on her own, from her first marriage. Nevertheless, Thomas felt it necessary to lay off some of his servants. Eventually, his children moved to their own properties.

He Kept His Pen Busy

This was supposed to be a restful period for Thomas, but he kept his pen busy. Not only did he finish his *Confutation,* but during 1532 and 1533 he wrote a "letter" and four books. Shortly after his retirement, a man by the name of John Frith, a scholar who wrote favorably about Lutheranism, thought it was safe to return to England. He miscalculated. Having declared himself head of the Catholic Church in England, King Henry couldn't be seen as condoning heresy. Therefore, he had Frith arrested and imprisoned in the Tower of London. There he wrote a treatise that denied the real presence of Christ in the Eucharist. Someone took a copy of the treatise to Thomas at Chelsea. After reading it, Thomas felt obliged to write a reply because the Catholic doctrine of the Eucharist was so important to him. The result is known as "Letter Against Frith." He called Frith's treatise "a false foolish treatise against the Blessed Sacrament of the Altar."

Thomas circulated the letter only to some of his friends after he wrote it in 1532, saying, "I would wish that the common people should of such heresies never hear so much as the name." (However, it was published at the end of 1533.) He wrote that the real presence of Christ in the Eucharist was a token of his Mystical Body on earth—the Catholic Church itself. Frith eventually was convicted of heresy and burned.

Near the end of 1532, Christopher St. German wrote an anonymous treatise in which he returned to his theme that English common law trumped canon law and must control church courts. Thomas replied with *The Apology of Sir Thomas More, Knight*, in which he not only refuted St. German but defended his own role as a defender of the Church. Thomas knew full well who wrote the anonymous treatise, but he took advantage of the fact that he was supposedly replying to an unknown author rather than to someone close to King Henry. He had pledged not to interfere in temporal matters, but surely he couldn't be criticized as a good Catholic who was defending his faith.

His *Apology* showed his frustration that so few Catholics seemed to be aware of the threats to their beliefs and practices. He felt quite alone while appealing to his "good Christian readers" to understand what was happening in England. He created an image of a Corpus Christi procession, bearing the Blessed Sacrament, which was attacked by a gang of hoodlums that threw the sacrament, relics, crosses and other things into the mire. He accused his unnamed adversary of willfully attempting to subvert the Catholic Church. He wrote that England "may fall so far down, down, down, down" that it might never rise again.

In his *Apology*, though, Thomas also denied the rumor that had circulated that he had flogged heretics against a tree in the garden of his home in Chelsea. It's true that he had interrogated suspects at his home and had held them in stocks, but he said that he had never whipped them, "as help me God." He was hardly accustomed to falsely invoking God's name, so there's no reason not to believe him.

The *Apology* was published in April of 1533. Soon thereafter, St. German wrote a reply, again anonymously, that he called *Salem and Bizance*. Published by the king's printer, it accused Thomas of bad faith and subterfuge, and of misrepresenting the processes of the law. By this time, it seemed that Thomas couldn't keep from writing. He composed his *Debellation of Salem and Bizance* within a few days and it was published in October. ("Debellation" meant "Destruction") He undoubtedly sensed, from other events that we'll consider soon, that he was losing the fight and he was determined to continue as long as possible.

St. German had accused the clergy of encouraging heresy by their treatment of heretics, an argument that Thomas couldn't accept. He replied that the unknown author was blaming the clergy for his supporters' actions. He noted that a statue of Saint Thomas Becket on London Bridge had recently been torn down and defaced by followers of the heresies. Up to this time, Thomas Becket had been a favorite saint of the English people and Thomas himself had a special devotion to his namesake.

As soon as he finished that book, he started on still another. After John Frith had been burned at the stake, another anonymous tract appeared defending Frith's approach to the Eucharist. Called *The Supper of the Lord*, it also denied the Catholic doctrine of the real presence in the Eucharist, labeling the Eucharist as only a meal of remembrance. Thomas replied with *The Answer to a Poisoned Book*, which he published in December along with the earlier private "Letter Against Frith."

In *The Answer to a Poisoned Book*, Thomas ridiculed the author of the other book as a "Master Masker" who hid behind the mask of anonymity (although he, too, had done so when he wrote his *Response to Luther*). He wrote that a mask *hides* the reality of the human person while the Eucharist *discloses* the reality of the Christian's incorporation into the Mystical Body of Christ. Christ's presence in the Eucharist, therefore, was real and not just a symbol.

ANNE BOLEYN IS CROWNED QUEEN

While Thomas was writing his books in his library at Chelsea, other events were beginning to catch up with him. After Archbishop Warham of Canterbury died in 1532, Henry bypassed the entire episcopacy in England to nominate Thomas Cranmer as Archbishop of Canterbury in 1533. At the time, Cranmer was Archdeacon of Taunton. He was also married, although that fact wasn't generally known.

Cranmer presided at the Convocation of Clergy that, in April of 1533, declared that the marriage of King Henry and Catherine was invalid. The convocation also forbade unauthorized preaching, and Bishop John Fisher was arrested, but eventually released. Then, on April 12, 1533, Anne Boleyn was declared Queen of England.

She and Henry had secretly married a week before Parliament had opened in February and Anne was already pregnant. In May Archbishop Cranmer pronounced the marriage to be valid. When Thomas learned about it, he said to William Roper, "God give grace, son Roper, that these matters within a while are not confirmed with oaths."

The coronation of the new queen in Westminster Abbey was the culmination of four days of festivities. Thomas did not attend and it's widely believed that it was at this point that Henry completely hardened his heart against him. Up to this time he had tolerated Thomas's known opposition, but he considered this to be a personal snub.

Thomas didn't attend despite the fact that three bishops, including his former colleague Cuthbert Tunstall, urged him, as a king's councilor, to be present. They even sent money to him to buy a new robe for the occasion. According to Roper, when Thomas next saw the three bishops he began by telling them a story of the emperor Tiberius who had enacted a law that exacted death for a certain crime unless the offender was a virgin. When a virgin did appear on that charge, he didn't know what to do. But then a member of his council said, "Why make so much ado, my lords, about so small a matter? Let her first be deflowered and after that she may be devoured."

After telling the story, Roper says that Thomas then told the bishops:

> And so, though your lordships have in the matter of
> the matrimony kept yourselves pure virgins, yet take
> good heed, my lords, that you keep your virginity
> still. For some there be that by procuring your lord-
> ships first at the coronation to be present, and next to
> preach for the setting forth of it, and finally to write
> books to all the world in defense thereof, are desir-
> ous to deflower you; and when they have deflowered
> you, then will they not fail soon after to devour you.
> Now, my lords, it lies not in my power but that they
> may devour me. But God, being my good Lord, will
> provide that they shall never deflower me!

THOMAS AND THE HOLY MAID OF KENT

A month after Queen Anne's coronation, Thomas visited Elizabeth Barton. She was known either as the Holy Maid of Kent or the Mad Nun of Kent, depending upon one's point of view. She first gained attention in 1525 when, as a seventeen-year-old servant in a Kent household, she began to prophesy during an illness. Her trances and visions continued and she came to the attention of church leaders, including Cardinal Wolsey. It was generally believed that her visions and claimed visitations were authentic. Bishop John Fisher was among those who believed her. She was admitted to a convent as a nun where her prophecies took on a political nature. She warned King Henry that he would die if he divorced Catherine and that Princess Mary would become queen.

Most of England was aware of Barton, including, of course, Thomas More. At one point, in fact, while Thomas was still Lord Chancellor, the king had shown him a roll of paper containing rhymed prophecies. Thomas had discreetly told the king that the woman's trances meant nothing that he could regard as anything but the work of a "right simple woman."

One of the nun's followers, Richard Risby of the Franciscan Observants at Canterbury, stayed with Thomas overnight and praised her. Thomas replied that he thanked God to hear of her good works, but when the subject matter turned to the king's marriage, he interrupted Risby to say that he would not hear of any revelation concerning the king.

However, as I noted above, Thomas visited the nun a month after Anne's coronation. They spoke alone in a private chapel. Later Thomas wrote, in a letter to Cromwell, that he told her that he did not come to hear her revelations but to ask for her prayers because he had heard of her virtue. According to Thomas, Barton replied that she knew well who he was and that she was already praying for him. She also told him about visitations she had had from the devil. However, Thomas insisted to Cromwell, "we talked no word of the King's Grace or any great personage else, nor in effect, of any man or woman but of herself and myself."

It's perfectly clear that Thomas was being as circumspect as possible. After he met with Barton, he wrote a letter to her, carefully keeping a copy for himself, confirming what they had discussed. He asked her to recall that "I showed you that I neither was, nor would be, curious of any knowledge of other men's matters, and least of all of any matter of princes or of the realm." He also refused to meet with her again. Twice she came to his home, but both times met only with Meg Roper and Giles Heron.

CROMWELL WAS OUT TO GET THOMAS

Thomas had every reason to be circumspect. He knew that Cromwell was investigating Barton for possible treason. Not only her, but also others close to Thomas, including Fathers Peto and Elstow, both of whom had fled England and were now living in Antwerp. Investigators learned that a merchant in London was financing the two priests, and it's possible that he could have been Antonio Bonvisi, Thomas's close friend who had recently been godfather for Thomas's latest grandchild, John More's second child. (He had married Anne Cresacre, Thomas's ward.) One of Cromwell's spies reported that he had learned that Thomas had sent to Father Peto copies of the books he had written against Tyndale and Frith, among other books.

Thomas knew by this time that Cromwell was out to get him, too. One day, as the family sat down for dinner, there was a knock at the door. A messenger from the king demanded that Thomas appear immediately before the royal commissioners. Thomas watched as some members of the household wept while others maintained their dignity. Then he admitted that there was no summons. He had devised the scene to see how his family would react, but also to prepare them for the ordeal he was convinced was to come soon. He hadn't been able to tell his family, even his wife, that he had been lying awake at night while Alice slept beside him, worrying about how he would react to tortures and the possibility of a painful death.

In July of 1533, Pope Clement VII, in solemn consistory, formally condemned King Henry's separation from Catherine and threatened him with excommunication if he did not return to her. One of Henry's reactions was to have Elizabeth Barton and her closest associates arrested, charging her with treason. The new Lord Chancellor, Thomas Audley, accused her of being responsible for the pope's position on Henry's marriage. After lengthy interrogation, Barton was taken to Paul's Cross, where she stood on a scaffold and admitted that her revelations and visitations had been fraudulent.

Soon after the nun's "confession," the king's council published a book of *Articles* that condemned Henry's excommunication from the Catholic Church while proclaiming the autonomy of the kingdom. It called the pope a "bastard, simoniac and heretic." Two or three weeks later, a reply appeared. Cromwell immediately suspected Thomas. He went to William Rastell and questioned him about Thomas's possible involvement in the reply. Rastell denied that Thomas had written, or that he had published, the reply. Afterward, he asked Thomas to write to Cromwell to back him up.

Thomas did write to Cromwell. He denied writing the reply, saying that, of the things touched upon in the *Articles*, "in some I know not the law, and in some I know not the fact. And therefore would I never be so childish nor so play the proud arrogant fool as to presume to make an answer to the book." Cromwell probably still did not believe him.

THOMAS IS ACCUSED OF BEING AN ACCOMPLICE OF ELIZABETH BARTON

After Parliament convened in 1534, Elizabeth Barton was indicted on charges of treason. A bill was introduced in Parliament, at the insistence of King Henry, which included the names of Thomas and Bishop Fisher as her accomplices. Thomas was accused of "misprision of treason," or concealment of treason, because he knew about Barton's treasonable actions. William Roper, who was still a member of the House of Commons, said that Cromwell told him that Thomas had communication with Barton and had given her advice and council.

This was serious business. Thomas immediately sent a lengthy letter to Cromwell in which he detailed all of his transactions with the woman he now called "the lewd nun." After receiving the letter, Cromwell asked Thomas to meet with him. By this time it seems likely that Cromwell was convinced that Thomas had not been colluding with Barton. He really wanted to talk with Thomas about the king's marriage to Anne and the issue of papal supremacy. Thomas repeated what he had said so often, that he consistently had maintained a policy of silence about the king's marital affairs. As for papal supremacy, he cleverly told Cromwell that he hadn't been convinced of the pope's supremacy until he read King Henry's treatise on the seven sacraments, in which the divine origin of the papacy was asserted.

After returning to Chelsea, the lawyer in him told Thomas to confirm their discussions with a follow-up letter. He repeated, concerning the king's marriage, "I neither murmur at it, nor dispute upon it, nor never did nor will." He also sent a letter to Henry, protesting his inclusion in the bill before Parliament. He said that he could not be capable of such "monstrous ingratitude" toward him as to conspire against him, and asked him to "relieve the torment of my present heaviness, conceived of the dread and fear" of seeing his name on that bill. He signed the letter "Your most humble and most heavy faithful subject and beadman." (A "beadman" is one who says the rosary for someone's intentions.)

A MEETING WITH A COMMITTEE OF THE STAR CHAMBER

Henry apparently didn't believe Thomas because, when Cromwell urged the king to drop Thomas from the bill before

Parliament, he refused. However, he agreed to appoint a committee of the Star Chamber to meet with Thomas. The members of the committee were Cromwell, Archbishop Cranmer, Lord Chancellor Thomas Audley, and Thomas Howard, the Duke of Norfolk.

William Roper, who surely heard about the meeting shortly afterward, wrote in his biography of Thomas that the committee began by being very friendly, inviting Thomas to sit down with them. Thomas refused to do so. Audley then recounted the honors and privileges that the king had bestowed on Thomas and said that the king would have been happy to have had him remain in office. Thomas replied, "No man living is there that would with better will do the thing that should be acceptable to the King's Highness than I, which needs confess his manifold benefits, and bountiful goodness most benignly on me."

He continued, Roper wrote:

> I hoped that I should never have heard of this matter more, considering that I have from time to time always from the beginning so plainly and truly declared my mind to his Grace, which his Highness to me ever seemed, like a most gracious prince, very well to accept, never minding, as he said, to molest me more therewith. Since which time any further thing that was able to move me to any change could I never find, and if I could, there is none in all the world that could have been gladder of it than I.

That didn't satisfy the committee and, after more discussion, the mood turned hostile. The committee accused him of having, "by his subtle sinister sleights" while he was the king's secretary, to have influenced the king to write his book against Martin Luther and in favor of papal supremacy. Thomas denied it, saying that it was the king who convinced him, not the other way around. Then its members resorted to threats, to which

Thomas replied (in the words of Saint Basil when the Arian Emperor Valens tried to convert him with threats), "These terrors are the arguments for children, and not for me."

The meeting ended and Thomas joined his son-in-law in the boat that took them back to Chelsea. Roper noted that Thomas seemed "very merry" and hoped that it was because "he had gotten himself discharged out of the Parliament Bill." When they arrived home, they walked together in his garden and Roper reported this conversation:

> "Sir, I trust all is well, because you are so merry."
>
> "That is so, indeed, son Roper. I thank God," he said.
>
> "Are you put out of the Parliament Bill then?" said I.
>
> "By my truth, son Roper," he said, "I never remembered it."
>
> "Never remembered it, Sir?" I said. "A case that touches yourself so near, and all of us for your sake? I am sorry to hear it. For I verily trusted, when I saw you so merry, that all had been well."
>
> "Would you know, son Roper, why I was so merry?"
>
> "That I would gladly, sir."
>
> "In good faith, I rejoiced, son, that I had given the devil a foul fall; that with those lords I had gone so far as, without great shame, I could never go back again."

Thomas had acquitted himself quite well during the interrogation. He did not incriminate himself in any way and was able to remain faithful to King Henry. He had a right to feel merry.

A Temporary Reprieve

The House of Lords learned about Thomas's interrogation and sent a request to the king, asking that he and the others named in the Bill be called before the House of Lords to defend themselves. The request angered the king, who threatened to attend the proceedings in the House of Lords and coerce the lords. His councilors, however, talked him out of that for fear that the House of Lords would resist his efforts. So finally Henry agreed to drop Thomas's name from the bill. However, he stopped the income that Thomas had still been receiving as a king's councilor.

Cromwell made it a point to see William Roper in the Parliament chambers and give him the good news. Roper sent a messenger to Chelsea to tell Meg, who then told her father. He replied, "In faith, Meg, *quod differtur non aufertur* (what is deferred is not avoided)." He knew the king well enough to understand that he would find some other way to get him.

A member of the Star Chamber's committee, Thomas Howard, understood the same thing. According to Roper, he met with Thomas and told him,

> "By the Mass, Master More, it is perilous striving with princes, and therefore I would wish you somewhat to incline to the king's pleasure. For by God's body, Master More, *Indignatio principis mors est* (the wrath of the king means death)."
>
> "Is that all, my Lord?" he said. "Then in good faith there is no more difference between your grace and me, but that I shall die today and you tomorrow."

Thomas didn't have long to wait for the king's next move. Two weeks later the Act of Succession was put before the House of Lords. It declared the marriage between Henry and Catherine to be void and annulled. It further stated that no power on earth could sanction "prohibited" marriages, thus ending the authority of the pope. It then proclaimed the succession to the throne to be through the children of Queen Anne. It then ordered all of the king's subjects to "make a corporal oath" to maintain "the whole effects and contents of this present Act." Thomas's prediction had come true.

As this was going on, Thomas was, as usual, writing. But now his writing changed considerably. Rather than trying to defend the Catholic Church, he turned to spiritual meditation. He began to write *A Treatise on the Passion*, about the last days of Jesus' life. It's hard not to see this treatise as a preparation for his own death, but there were also numerous allusions to contemporary events as he described the Jewish elders as "worldly winning" but with "private malice" as they pretended "great zeal unto the commonwealth." As he meditated on Christ's passion, he prayed for the grace never to "give my assent to follow the sinful device of any wicked counsel."

However, *A Treatise on the Passion* was more than a meditation. Thomas clearly recognized that the Catholic Church was being destroyed in England, as it already had been damaged by Martin Luther in Germany and by other reformers in other countries. He foresaw the time when "it shall seem that there shall be no Christian countries left at all." Then, he believed, the Antichrist would appear. But his reign would be short and Christ would then come "and finish this present world, and reward every good man after his good works wrought in his true Catholic faith." Therefore, he exhorted his "good Christian readers" to stand firm in the faith.

Before he could put the final touches on *A Treatise on the Passion*, the moment came that he long had feared. He was summoned to take the oath of succession.

CHAPTER 10

TRIED AND IMPRISONED

I suppose we could consider Thomas as a model prisoner, as indeed he was, using his time to prepare for eternity. However, as I said in the Foreword, my plan was to offer him as a model mainly for the years before his imprisonment and death. Nevertheless, we can also follow his example of facing his fears with fortitude and keeping our eye always on the prize of eternal life, for which there is nothing in this life that can be more valuable.

Thomas was busy, during the end of March and first part of April of 1534, putting his life in order. Among other things, he prepared a "conveyance for the disposition of all his lands," according to Roper, bequeathing a portion of his estate to William and Meg. Then he went on pilgrimage to one of his favorite churches, Our Lady of Willesden. He stayed that time with his stepdaughter Alice, his wife Alice's daughter, and her husband, Sir Giles Alington. He obviously had *A Treatise on the Passion* on his mind because he sent his secretary some changes in that document while in the Alington home.

On Sunday, April 12, he attended Mass at St. Paul's before walking to his old home in Bucklersbury, where his adopted daughter Margaret Giggs now lived with her husband, John Clement. While he was there he was handed a summons to appear at Lambeth Palace the next day to take the oath of succession.

Thomas returned to Chelsea, told his family about the summons, and spent the night in prayer. On April 13, he went to his parish church where he went to confession, attended Mass and received Holy Communion. Returning home, he gathered his family in the garden. But let William Roper tell the story:

> Whereas he used always before, at his departure from his house and children (whom he loved tenderly) to have them bring him to his boat, and there to kiss them all, and bid them farewell, this time he would allow none of them to follow him out of the gate, but pulled the wicket after him and shut them all from him, and with a heavy heart (as by his countenance it appeared) with me, and our four servants, there took his boat towards Lambeth.
>
> Sitting sadly awhile, at last he rounded me in the ear and said, "Son Roper, I thank Our Lord, the field is won."
>
> What he meant thereby, I knew not. Yet loath to seem ignorant I answered, "Sir, I am thereof very glad." But as I conjectured afterward, it was for that the love he had to God wrought in him so effectually, that it conquered in him all his carnal affections utterly.

In other words, God had given him the grace to conquer his feelings for his family and he was certain that he would not betray his conscience for their sake. In closing the gate, he was certain that he would never see Chelsea again. He was right.

THOMAS REFUSES TO SWEAR THE OATH

What happened next was reported by Thomas himself in letters to his daughter Meg. He wrote that he was not the only person called to take the oath, but he was the only lay person called that day. He was led before Audley, Cromwell, Cranmer, and William Benson, the Abbot of Westminster and was asked if he was now ready to swear the oath. He asked to see a copy of it and was presented a small roll. After reading it carefully, he asked to see a copy of the Act of Succession, which he carefully compared to the oath. Finally he spoke out:

> My purpose is not to put any fault either in the Act or any man that made it, or in the oath or any man that swears it, nor to condemn the conscience of any other man. But as for myself in good faith, my conscience so moves me in the matter, that though I will not deny to swear to the succession, yet unto the oath that here is offered to me I cannot swear, without the jeopardizing of my soul to perpetual damnation.

Thomas undoubtedly had rehearsed what he was going to say and had, in fact, explained it to his wife Alice. He had no objection to the succession passing on to the children of Henry and Queen Anne, but he could not swear to an oath that denied the authority of the pope. At the time, Alice told him that God regards the heart rather than the tongue and that the meaning of the oath "goes upon what they think and not upon what they say." Thomas, though, did not believe that he could do that. Therefore, he continued his statement to his interrogators:

> If you doubt whether I do refuse the oath only for the grudge of my conscience, or any other fantasy, I am ready here to satisfy you by my oath. Which, if you do not trust it, why should you be the better to give me *any* oath? And if you trust that I will herein swear true, then I trust of your goodness you will not move me to swear the oath you had offered me, perceiving that for to swear it is against my conscience.

Audley then showed Thomas a printed roll with the signatures of the members of Parliament on it, saying that Thomas was the first to refuse to sign it—not quite true, since Bishop Fisher had also refused. Thomas simply repeated what he had said, that he couldn't swear to it but did not blame anyone else who did. The group then told him to take a walk in the garden to reflect or meditate and he would be recalled later.

Since it was a hot day for April, Thomas decided instead to wait in a room where he could see others arriving to sign the oath, some quite jovially. Later he called the parade a "pageant." One who refused to sign, Nicholas Wilson, was paraded before Thomas as he was being led to the Tower.

When he was recalled, he was asked what part of the oath he objected to. He replied that he obviously had offended the king already but had no wish to do so more. He adopted a strategy of silence, knowing that the law provided that no one was obliged to condemn himself. Cranmer told him that he had a certain duty to obey the king while his conscience was doubtful since it was different from that of others, but Thomas didn't find that reasoning persuasive. Abbot Benson told him that his conscience was opposed by so many of the clergy who had signed the oath, but Thomas replied that he could claim the support of "the general counsel of Christendom."

The meeting ended with Thomas repeating that he would swear to the succession but not to the oath, again invoking his conscience but refusing to give his reasons. Later, he told Meg that, in reading the Act and then the oath, he saw clearly that the oath went far beyond the succession, requiring him to accept "all other acts and statutes made since the beginning of the present Parliament," and this included much antipapal legislation.

Thomas was arrested and put in the custody of Abbot Benson, where he remained for the following four days. During that time, Cranmer wrote to Cromwell proposing that Thomas (and Bishop Fisher) be required to swear only to the Act of Succession and that this could be publicized widely. Cromwell took the possible compromise to the king, who turned it down flat. It might serve as a precedent, he said. It was all or nothing.

Therefore, on April 17, 1534, Thomas was sent to prison in the Tower of London. He had not lost his sense of humor. He was met by Sir Edmund Walsingham, the lieutenant of the Tower, and a porter. It was the custom for the porter to ask for "the upper garment" of new prisoners. When he did so, Thomas gave him his hat. "No, sir," the porter said. "I must have your gown."

Walsingham took him to his cell, or chamber, and asked him to accept it in as much cheer as possible, to which Thomas is said to have replied, "If any here like it not, turn him out of doors."

As the most distinguished "guest" of the Tower, Thomas was given a cell better than most. His five-sided room built of thick stones measured about eighteen feet by twenty feet, with a vaulted ceiling nineteen feet high. The floor had uneven stones and the windows were slits. He had a bed, table and chair and a small brick stove. One of his own servants, John Wood, was permitted to attend to him, and he did throughout Thomas's imprisonment. Thomas was permitted to walk in the gardens and even enjoy the king's menagerie that was kept there. He was also able to attend Mass daily.

Left alone in his cell, though, he continued to experience the fears he had had before his imprisonment, but to an even greater extent. Naturally, he worried about his family and how they would be able to fare, but he worried especially about whether or not he would persevere or would eventually give up and sign the oath. He considered the torture that he might have to endure and confessed in a letter that he thought "my flesh much more shrinking from pain and from death that I thought it the part of a faithful Christian man."

King Henry made sure that Thomas thought about it. Three days after his imprisonment, Elizabeth Barton and five priests who had supported her were taken from their cells in the Tower and tied to wooden planks. Horses then dragged the planks five miles through the cobbles, stones and mud to Tyburn, where they were executed. Barton had the easiest death. She was hanged, the executioner pulling on her legs until she was dead. The priests suffered more cruelly. Each was hanged first, but after he lost consciousness he was revived so he could watch while his penis was cut off and stuffed in his mouth, his stomach was cut open and his intestines thrown into boiling water, and his heart was plucked from his body and held before his face. (According to Alan Neame's book *The Holy Maid of Kent*, one of the priests cried, "What you are holding is consecrated to God.") Finally they were beheaded, their heads parboiled and placed on pikes on London Bridge. This, as Thomas was well aware, was the usual penalty for treason, as burning at the stake had been the penalty for heresy.

MAKING PRISON HIS MONASTERY

During the first part of his imprisonment, Thomas was not permitted to have visitors. Therefore, he organized his life as if he were in a cell in the Charterhouse where he once lived. He had his New Testament, Psalter and Book of Hours as well as other devotional books. He prayed and sang the Liturgy of the Hours. He penned marginal notes in his prayer books to aid his meditations. He wrote that he meditated particularly on the testing of St. Peter, the martyrdom of St. Stephen, and the passion of Christ. He continued to wear the hair shirt he had worn most of his life and it was reported that he whipped himself for penance. He no longer shaved or cut his hair, emulating Pope Benedict XIII who, while imprisoned at Avignon, vowed not to cut his beard until he was released. Thomas, though, did not expect to be released.

Thomas had had a love of the psalms all of his life, and now he selected some of them that he prayed regularly—psalms twenty, twenty-two, seventy-four, ninety-eight, and one hundred eleven. He also collected verses from thirty-one psalms to form one powerful prayer. He called this prayer "Imploring Divine Help against Temptation, While Scorning Demons through Hope and Confidence in God." When Meg was permitted to visit him, they always began their visit by reciting the seven penitential psalms.

Before she was permitted to visit her father, Meg wrote him a letter in which she urged him to swear the oath, as she herself had done. That letter no longer exists, but apparently she tried as persuasively as she could to convince him, and she said that he was in prison because "of the scruple" of his conscience. Thomas wrote later that the letter deeply wounded him "surely far above all other things" since he wasn't able to convince his own beloved daughter that he had to follow his conscience.

When, after about a month, Meg, and only Meg, was permitted to visit him, he told her that, of all God's favors to him, he considered his imprisonment "the very chief" because he was able to withdraw completely from the world and prepare for eternity without the fear of a sudden and unexpected death. He also repeated for her his belief in the unity of the Catholic Church and the Communion of Saints. He gave her a formal letter "to all my loving friends" in effect giving her his power of attorney.

Besides not being permitted visitors at first, Thomas also was not given pen and ink. Therefore, his first letter to Meg was written with a piece of coal. However, the notations in his Psalter and Book of Hours are written in ink, as are subsequent letters.

Thirteen of Thomas's prison letters still survive, eight written to Meg and five to friends. We know that Thomas exchanged letters with Bishop Fisher, who was being kept in another part of the Tower. The letters were carried by George Golde, the Tower lieutenant's servant, who burned the letters after they were read. They would not have been of a compromising nature, because surely the lieutenant would have read them, but simply encouraged one another and offered prayers for each other. Thomas said that they had discussed the "king's matter" only once, Thomas saying that he had not sworn the oath but refusing to say anything further.

THOMAS'S *DIALOGUE OF COMFORT AGAINST TRIBULATION*

With plenty of time on his hands, Thomas set about writing a lengthy treatise that he called *A Dialogue of Comfort Against Tribulation*. Some people believe that it is his greatest masterpiece. It was a mixture of narrative and fable, filled with recollections of his past life and of the people who were important parts of his life. He took the word "comfort" as a derivative of the Latin *fortis*, meaning strong, and he showed how it was possible to endure hardships and approaching death.

He created a story set in Hungary in 1527 or 1528, after the first invasion by the Turk's Suleiman the Magnificent and just prior to the second devastating battle. The "dialogue" in the title was between an elderly man named Antony, lying sick in bed, and his nephew, Vincent, the young leader of the Hungarians. Their city, Buda, is surrounded by Suleiman's troops and the two men try to find comfort in their tribulation. Vincent is terrified, not only for himself but for his family and those who must fight the Turks. Vincent knows that he could preserve his status by making some compromises and he has come to Antony for counsel. Through their dialogue, which consists of three conversations, Vincent makes a translation from paralyzing fear to trust in God. The similarity with Thomas's predicament was obvious.

The treatise was written as three books, with tribulation considered from the perspective of faith in the first book, hope in the second, and charity in the third. By the end, Thomas

showed that, only when the human emotions of fear are overcome by the promise of eternal life can the mind be redeemed
by faith, the memory and imagination by hope, and the heart
by charity.

That's the gist of the book, but it takes a long time to reach
the conclusion. Thomas does it through lengthy conversations
that are interspersed, at times, with humorous tales, and at other
times with strange stories. One of the strange stories concerned
a woman who wanted a neighbor to behead her so that she
would, somehow, be taken as a martyr. (Several stories concern
beheadings, obviously on Thomas's mind.) But she also wanted
the bloody axe to be taken to another neighbor's house so that
that neighbor would be charged with murder.

Another tale was about a man who, on a Good Friday,
wanted to be crucified like Christ and asked his wife to help. She
reminded him that Christ first was scourged and crowned with
thorns, so first she tied him up and beat him. Then, while she
was weaving a crown of thorns, her husband decided that "this
was enough for this year" and they would resume when Good
Friday came again. A year later he had changed his mind.

During one of the conversations, Vincent suggests that it
might be best for him not to think about the coming peril. Antony, however, advises the opposite: The best comfort, he says, is
to meditate long and often about the nature of the sufferings in
order to acquire "such a sure habit of spiritual faithful strength
that all the devils in hell, with all the wrestling that they can
make, shall never be able to wrest it" from one's heart. That,
obviously, was Thomas's belief and hope.

He thought about martyrdom, too, but he realized that it
would be a form of spiritual pride to consider himself worthy of
such a death. He had stories about those with a desire to commit
suicide, too, with Antony telling Vincent that it's sometimes
necessary to bind the suicidal person in bed until the temptation
passes. Then, once the temptation has passed, the person must
rely on whatever comforts he can find—encouragement from

others, the sacrament of Penance, and meditation on the truths of the faith. The book ends with a lengthy meditation on the passion of Christ. By remembering the example of Christ, Vincent finally is able to live up to his name as "one who conquers."

ALICE'S VISIT WITH HER HUSBAND

Throughout Thomas's imprisonment, his wife Alice couldn't understand what had come over him, why he was being so obstinate. Finally, after a long period of time, she was permitted to visit him. In his biography, William Roper related the conversation:

> At her first coming like a simple woman, and somewhat worldly too, she bluntly saluted him, "Master More, I marvel that you, who have always been taken for such a wise man, should now so play the fool as to lie here in this close, filthy prison, and be content to be shut up among mice and rats, when you might be about and at your liberty, and with the favor and good will both of the king and his council, if you would but do as all the bishops and best learned of this realm have done. And seeing you have at Chelsea a right fair house, your library, your books, your gallery, your garden, your orchards, and all other necessaries so handsomely about you, where you might, in the company of me your wife, your children, and household be merry, I muse what in God's name you mean here still this fondly to tarry."
>
> After he had a while quietly heard her, with a cheerful countenance he said to her, "I pray you, good Mistress Alice, tell me one thing."
> "What is that?" she asked.
> "Is not this house as near heaven as my own?"

To whom she, after her accustomed fashion, not liking such talk, answered, *"Tille valle tille valle."* (Tille valle, derived from the name of the demon Tityvillus, was the phrase for idle talk.)

"How say you, Mistress Alice, is it not so?" he asked.

"Bone Deus, bone Deus, man, will you never stop repeating the same things?" she said.

"But, Mistress Alice, if it be so, it is very well."

He went on to say that he saw no reason why he should enjoy his house or anything in it when, if he should be buried for seven years and then rise again and find someone else in his house, they would tell him to be gone since none of it was his. "What cause have I then to like such a house as would so soon forget his master?" he asked.

As Alice continued to emphasize the possibility of a long life outside of prison, Thomas asked, "How long, my Alice, shall I be able to enjoy this life?"

"A full twenty years, if God so wills."

"Do you wish me, then, to exchange eternity for twenty years? Here, good wife, you do not bargain very skillfully."

LORD CHANCELLOR AUDLEY INTERVENES

In August of 1534, Lord Chancellor Thomas Audley arrived at the estate of Sir Giles Alington and his wife Alice, Thomas's stepdaughter, ostensibly to hunt. While there, he invited Alice to visit him at the nearby home of his father-in-law. Alice was happy to do so "because I would speak to him for my father."

Audley seems to have had a sincere interest in trying to help Thomas. He said, "I marvel that your father is so obstinate in his own conceit, as that everybody went forth with all save only the blind bishop (Fisher) and he." He then told Alice two stories that he called Aesop's fables. The first was about the folly of thinking yourself over-wise, while the second concerned the perils of an excessively scrupulous conscience.

After this meeting, Alice immediately wrote to her half-sister, Meg, and related the conversation she had had with Audley. The next time Meg was permitted to visit Thomas, she gave him Alice's letter, telling him that he was likely to lose all the friends who were able to do him any good. Thomas replied, "What, Mistress Eve, has my daughter Alice played the serpent with you and with a letter set you at work to come tempt your father again?" (Once earlier he had called her Eve because she was trying to tempt him.)

After her visit, Meg sent a lengthy letter to Alice with the details of the visit. The letter, though, appears to have been written by Thomas or, perhaps, by Thomas and Meg together. It includes Meg's arguments to try to persuade (tempt?) her father, and his replies. Thomas insisted, in two long sentences,

> that if it were possible in this matter for me to do the thing that might content the King's Grace without God being offended, there is no man who has already taken this oath more gladly than I would do, as one who reckons himself more deeply bound unto the King's Highness for his most singular bounty, many ways showed and declared, than any of them all beside. But since, standing by my conscience, I can in no wise do it, and that for the instruction of my conscience in the matter I have not slightly looked, but by many years studied and advisedly considered, and never could yet see or hear that thing, and I think I never shall, that could induce my own mind to think otherwise than I do, I have no manner of remedy.

Meg urged him to seriously consider the message she had

brought for "your tender friend and very good lord," Thomas
Audley. Thomas read it carefully, three times in fact, and said
he was grateful for Audley's concern but he couldn't agree with
the conclusions in Audley's two fables.

The first of Audley's "Aesop's fables" was about a country
inhabited mostly by fools. A storm came up and a few wise men
hid in caves until it passed, while the fools stayed in the rain.
Then the wise men came out of the caves expecting to be able
to rule the fools, but the fools rejected them. So the wise men
wished they had remained in the rain. Thomas's reaction was
surprise that anyone would want to rule fools. And certainly,
he said, he never longed to be a ruler.

The second fable concerned a lion and an ass that went
to confession. The lion confessed that he had devoured all the
beasts he could. The confessor absolved him because it was the
lion's nature to devour beasts. The ass confessed that he took
a straw from his master's shoe and that resulted in his master
catching cold. The confessor said that he couldn't absolve such
a sin and sent him to a bishop. Audley had concluded the fable
by saying, "I would not have your father so scrupulous of his
conscience."

After reading the fable, Thomas remarked that it couldn't
be by Aesop since he lived in Greece before the time of Christ,
when there were no confessions. He then took the reference to
the ass as being a charge that he was relying on the judgment
of Bishop Fisher. He denied that he would act on the judgment
of any other man. He said that he could not condemn any other
man for following his conscience if it didn't agree with his, but
he was responsible for his own conscience and could not follow
that of someone else. He assured her, "For your comfort I shall
say to you, daughter, that my own conscience in this matter (I
damn no other man's) is such as may well stand with my own
salvation. Of this I am, Meg, as sure as that God is in heaven."

Meg tried other arguments, telling him at one point that
she herself had sworn the oath. To which Thomas laughed and

said, "That word was like Eve too, for she offered Adam no worse fruit than she had eaten herself."

Meg reminded him that Parliament was still in session and could pass a law that could end in his death. Thomas replied, as a lawyer, "that if they would make a law to do me any harm, that law could never be lawful." As for his possible death, he told her, "During many a restless night, Margaret, while my wife slept and thought that I slept too, I counted what peril could possibly fall to me, so much so that I am sure that nothing more could come."

He concluded by telling her:

> Never trouble your mind over anything that ever shall happen to me in this world. Nothing can come but what God wills. And I make myself very sure that whatsoever that be, even if it seems ever so bad at sight, it shall indeed be the best…. And if anything happens to me that you would not approve, pray to God for me, but trouble not yourself: as I shall full heartily pray for us all that we may meet together in heaven where we shall be merry forever and never have trouble again.

By the time Meg took Alice's letter to him, Thomas was suffering from the effects of his imprisonment. He continued to have chest pains, as he had had prior to his confinement, but now he also complained of kidney stones and severe leg cramps. In a letter he had sent to another prisoner, Nicholas Wilson, he revealed that he twice had thought he was going to die. For the cold weather, Thomas's friend Antonio Bonvisi sent him a gown as well as some meat and drink.

PARLIAMENT ACCUSED THOMAS OF SEDITION

Meg had warned her father during her visit that Parliament was still in session. Indeed it was. The seventh session of the so-called "Reformation" Parliament convened in November of 1534 and immediately began to enact legislation that gave King Henry VIII more power. An Act of Supremacy proclaimed him to be "the only supreme head in earth of the Church of England." Another act required the Church to give a tenth of its income to the king. A Treason Act made it an offense, punishable by death, to "maliciously wish, will, or desire, by words or writing" to deprive the royal family of their "dignity, title or name of their royal estates," or to declare the king "heretic, schismatic, tyrant, infidel." Finally, two Acts of Attainder were passed, one directed at Bishop John Fisher and the other at Thomas More. The second accused him of "intending to sow sedition" by refusing the oath of succession. It further denounced him for having "unkindly and ungratefully served our sovereign lord by divers and sundry ways."

With the passage of that last act, the king was able to confiscate Thomas's manors and estates. Lady Alice tried to prevent that if she could. She wrote a letter directly to King Henry begging him to "pardon your most grievous displeasure to the said Sir Thomas" who was "in great continual sickness of body and heaviness of heart." Thomas would not have appreciated the letter had he known about it because she expressed the opinion of the family that his stubbornness was "a long continued and deep-rooted scruple, as passes his power to avoid and put away."

Alice also wrote in her letter to the king that she would be "utterly undone" if Thomas's lands and homes were confiscated. The letter had no effect on the king, and the lands and homes were confiscated, but we're not sure how impoverished the family became. Alice herself still owned estates that she inherited from her first husband. Thomas's children, stepdaughter and adopted daughter were all married to successful men. There are also indications that the family had moved any valuables out of the home in Chelsea. After Thomas's death, his son John became responsible for his debts, but other members of the family probably helped pay them.

With the passage of the Bill of Attainder against him, the last act was about to begin.

CHAPTER 11

CONVICTED AND EXECUTED

Thomas realized that he had no chance of winning his trial, but that didn't prevent him from arguing the case to the best of his legal abilities. Legal scholars have said through the centuries that he should have been found innocent. Having been condemned to death, he went to his execution joyfully, forgiving those who had convicted him and praying that they would meet again in heaven. Even at the time of his death, he was reminding us of our obligation to forgive those who have offended us.

At about the time of the passage of the Bill of Attainder, Thomas was apparently moved from the cell where he had been kept to another because he wrote to Meg that he was in "close keeping." He also warned her that there would probably be some sudden searches of his homes. For a time, at least, he didn't have the freedom he had had to move about outside his cell and he was prevented from attending daily Mass. He also was denied visitors again.

Alone in his cell, he again fell back to his writing. It would be his last work except for some meditations and prayers. This, too, though, was a meditation, *On the Sadness, Weariness, Fear and Prayer of Christ before His Passion*, usually referred to as *The Sadness of Christ*. Writing in Latin again, he pictured Christ's agony in the garden of Gethsemane, where he was overcome by fear and sadness to such an extent that his sweat fell like drops of blood.

In his meditation, Thomas asked how it could have been "that Christ himself, the very prototype and leader of martyrs, the standard bearer of them all, should [have been] so terrified at the approach of pain, so shaken, so utterly downcast?" His answer was that Christ willingly allowed his human nature to react to what was to come in order to teach us how to face our fears. Fear is normal, he wrote. It "is not reprehensible as long as reason does not cease to struggle against fear—a struggle which is not criminal or sinful but rather an immense opportunity for merit." It's easy to see the emotions Thomas was experiencing there in his cell.

One of those emotions was undoubtedly the feeling of being abandoned. All his life Thomas had been gregarious. He liked to be with people and to "be merry" with them. Now even his old friend Erasmus seems to have deserted him, although he didn't know about Erasmus's later remark, "If only he had left theology to the theologians!" Therefore, Thomas wrote about the three times that Jesus came to his apostles, only to find them sleeping. However, he wrote, "Judas the traitor at the same time was so wide awake and intent on betraying the Lord that the very idea of sleep never entered his head."

The apostles, Thomas wrote, were like the English bishops who also fell asleep during the destruction of their Church. He wrote:

> Does not this contrast between the traitor and the apostles present to us a clear and sharp mirror image (as it were), a sad and terrible view of what has happened through the ages from those times even to our own? Why do not bishops contemplate in this scene their own somnolence? Since they have succeeded in the place of the apostles, would that they would reproduce their virtues just as eagerly as they display their sloth and sleepiness!

What, then, does Thomas advise? Prayer. The apostles were sleeping while Jesus was praying, he wrote, because they had not yet developed the habit of prayer. While describing the scene where Jesus was praying that his "cup" might pass, Thomas addressed his readers directly, writing, "Reader, let us pause for a little at this point and contemplate with a devout mind our commander lying on the ground in humble supplication."

Christ was totally absorbed in his prayer, he wrote, while "we scratch our heads, clean our fingernails with a pocketknife, and pick our noses with our fingers, meanwhile making the wrong responses." He told his readers to imagine that they had committed a crime of high treason and were standing before a prince who had the power to commute or cancel the death penalty.

> Now when you have been brought into the presence of the prince, go ahead and speak to him carelessly, casually, without the least concern. Yawn, stretch, sneeze, spit without giving it a thought, and belch up the fumes of your gluttony. In short, conduct yourself in such a way that he can clearly see from your face, your voice, your gestures, and your whole bodily deportment that while you are addressing him you are thinking about something else. Tell me now, what success could you hope for from such a plea as this?

Jesus' example, Thomas wrote, was once more demonstrated when Judas and the soldiers appeared. As a result of his prayer he was able to endure his final agony with "manly courage." He has changed from a man who was so fearful and sad to one "who fearlessly approaches the whole mass of armed men." His prayer has enabled him to face heroically all that was to come. The meditation ended with the soldiers taking Jesus into custody and the apostles abandoning him.

The Sadness of Christ was written on one hundred fifty-five sheets of paper, about fifteen lines on each sheet. The sheets were smuggled out of the Tower, probably several pages at a time. The edges of some of the pages have been worn away and it's believed that these might be sheets that Thomas put into his pocket when his books and writing materials were taken away from him.

Besides *The Sadness of Christ*, Thomas also wrote several short treatises including *A Treatise on Receiving the Blessed Body, Imploring Divine Help against Temptation, A Godly Instruction on How to Treat Those Who Wrong Us, A Godly Meditation on Saving One's Life,* and *A Godly Meditation on Detachment.*

ANOTHER MEETING WITH CROMWELL

In the spring of 1535, John Haughton, prior of the London Charterhouse where Thomas had once lived, and the priors of two other Carthusian monasteries were arrested and interrogated by Thomas Cromwell. When they refused to swear an oath to accept King Henry as head of the Church of England they were condemned to death in the usual manner.

Two days later, on May 7, Thomas was summoned to meet with Cromwell and four others in a room at the Tower. We know what happened from a letter he subsequently wrote to Meg. It had been a while since he had previously seen Cromwell and the latter was probably surprised at Thomas's emaciated appearance. Cromwell invited him to sit with them, but Thomas refused. He was asked if he had read Parliament's new statutes, including the one that confirmed Henry as supreme head of the Church in England. Thomas acknowledged that he had. When asked his opinion about it, he replied as he had previously—that he had declared his mind to Henry himself in the past but now he had reserved his life for prayer alone and refused to meddle in such matters.

Cromwell told him that the king was quite willing to show him mercy and release him from prison, but Thomas replied simply, "My whole study shall be upon the passion of Christ."

Cromwell then sent him out of the room while the five men deliberated about what should be done in this difficult case. Eventually he was recalled.

Asked if he shouldn't be subject to parliamentary statutes like any other man, Thomas replied, "I will not say the contrary."

Cromwell then told him that one of the reasons he was imprisoned was because his "demeanor" in the matter was encouraging others to follow his example. It was clear that he was referring to the three Carthusian priors and Cromwell was implying that Thomas was indirectly responsible for their deaths. That aroused Thomas and he expressed his indignation forcefully:

> I do nobody harm, I say none harm, I think none harm, but wish everybody good. And if this isn't enough to keep a man alive, in good faith I long not to live. And I am dying already, and have since I came here, been divers times in the case that I thought to die within one hour, and I thank our Lord I was never sorry for it, but rather sorry when I saw the pain pass. And therefore my poor body is at the king's pleasure, would God my death might do him good.

Thomas wrote to Meg that Cromwell was gentler toward him after that. After a few more questions, he was sent back to his cell.

EXECUTION OF THE THREE PRIORS

Shortly after Meg received the letter, Alice wrote to Cromwell, the king's secretary, asking for an audience with the king so she could personally plead for her husband. Cromwell didn't answer the letter, but did permit Meg to have another visit with her father. It certainly was no coincidence that the visit coincided with the execution of the three Carthusian friars. Thomas and Meg couldn't see much out the slits that served as windows, but they could hear what was happening as the men were tied to hurdles and then dragged by horses to their execution at Tyburn.

As this was happening, Thomas said to Meg, as reported later by Roper, "Do you not see, Meg, that these blessed fathers are now as cheerful going to their deaths as bridegrooms to their marriages?" He then grieved that, speaking of himself, "God, thinking him not worthy so soon to come to that eternal felicity, leaves him here yet, still in the world further to be plunged and turmoiled with misery."

His death, though, was coming ever nearer. On June 3, 1535 he was called before a special commission that included Cromwell and Audley. Once again he was asked to give a plain answer regarding the oath of supremacy, which he refused to do. He said that he could neither speak in favor of the statute "against my conscience to the loss of my soul, or against it to the destruction of my body." In making that statement, though, he used the simile of a two-edged sword and it happened that Bishop John Fisher used the same simile. The commission, therefore, suspected collusion or at least communication between the two prisoners. Thus it was discovered that messages had been passed between the two men, but that the messages had been destroyed.

A Fateful Conversation with Richard Rich

On June 12, Richard Rich, the solicitor general, went to Thomas's cell with orders to confiscate all of his books and writing materials. With him were Sir Richard Southwell, a friend of Thomas's who might have intended to take the materials to Chelsea, a man named Thomas Palmer, and two servants. While Southwell and the servants were packing up the books, Rich struck up a conversation with Thomas. The men knew one another most of their lives and both were prominent lawyers. It was a fateful conversation.

After leaving Thomas's cell, Rich immediately went to Cromwell and reported the conversation. The two men had discussed hypothetical cases, he said, and along the way Thomas had denied that Parliament had the right to name the king supreme head of the Church. Of course, Thomas had done no such thing.

As for Thomas, once his books and writing materials were taken away, he asked for the windows of his cell to be covered. It was as though he was already in a tomb.

Two days later there was still another interrogation. This was a formal one, conducted by two official investigators with two other witnesses and a notary. Obviously, Thomas knew, this was in preparation for his trial. Asked if he would obey the king as supreme head of the Church in England, he replied, "I can make no answer." Would he accept Henry's marriage to Anne Boleyn as lawful? "I have never spoken against it, nor thereunto can make no answer." Didn't he think he was obliged to answer that first question? "I can make no answer." He continued to pursue a strategy of silence.

On June 17 John Fisher was tried for treason and condemned to death. He was now Cardinal Fisher since Pope Paul III had appointed him a cardinal at the end of May. On June 22 he was awakened at five o'clock in the morning with the news that he would be executed at nine o'clock. He asked to be allowed to sleep a little longer. He rose at seven and put on a clean white shirt and a fur cape because, he said, it was his wedding day. Since he was so frail and weak, it was obvious that he could not survive being dragged to Tyburn on a hurdle, so King Henry changed the sentence to that of beheading on Tower Hill.

He was carried to the hill. Opening a copy of the New Testament at random, he read a passage from the Gospel of St. John. He sang the *Te Deum* while climbing the scaffold. He took off his gown and the crowd gasped at his emaciated body. One blow easily separated his head from his body and an unusually large amount of blood gushed out. Then, as the king had demanded, his naked body was displayed on the scaffold while his head was thrust on a pike and placed in an iron cage on London Bridge. There it somehow became ruddy and comely until Henry ordered it thrown into the river.

The Most Famous Trial Since that of Socrates

Then it was Thomas's turn. His trial has been called the most famous trial since that of Socrates. On July 1, 1535 he appeared in Westminster Hall before fifteen judges and twelve jurors. To say that the court was stacked against him would be an understatement. Among the judges were Cromwell, Audley and Howard as well as Anne Boleyn's father, uncle and brother. In accordance with the custom at that time, he was not permitted counsel or a written account of the charges against him. Nevertheless, Thomas conducted his own defense with all his legal skill. This time, though, he had to sit rather than stand. After fifteen months in prison, he was weak physically but his mental powers were intact.

He was charged with four counts of treason: First, he refused to accept the royal supremacy at the meeting with the king's commission on May 7. Second, he was in collusion with a convicted traitor, Cardinal Fisher, and letters passed between them. Third, he had stirred up sedition by describing the Act of Supremacy as a two-edged sword. Fourth, in a conversation with Richard Rich, he had "maliciously, traitorously, and diabolically" denied that Parliament had the authority to declare the king the head of the Church in England.

Thomas managed to refute the first three charges by showing that no offense was involved in any of them. He had remained silent concerning that statute at the meeting on May 7, he said, and silence not only wasn't a crime but, according to

English precedent, it implied consent, not dissent. As for the letters, none of them concerned matters of state, he said, and, besides, since the letters no longer existed, there could be no evidence of treasonous activity. As for the charge concerning a two-edged sword, he said that he had spoken hypothetically and not maliciously. He had said that *if* the statute was like a two-edged sword forcing someone to choose between physical and spiritual life, the statute might later be considered illegitimate.

Thomas also denied the fourth charge, stating forcefully that Rich had committed perjury, but the trial focused on that charge, seeming to ignore the others. Rich was called to the stand and he repeated that, while Thomas's books were being removed and the two men engaged in conversation, Thomas had denied Parliament's right to name the king as head of the Church in England.

Thomas immediately went on the offensive, delivering this powerful testimony:

> If I were a man, my lords, who did not reverence an oath, I need not, as is well known, stand here as an accused person in this place, at this time, or in this case. And if this oath of yours, Master Rich, be true, then I pray that I never see God in the face, which I would not say, were it otherwise, to win the whole world.

He then tried to undermine Rich's credibility as a witness:

> In good faith, Master Rich, I am sorrier for your perjury than for my own peril. And you shall understand that neither I nor any other man to my knowledge ever took you to be a man of credit in any matter of importance that I or any other would at any time

design to communicate with you. And I, as you know, for no small while have been acquainted with you and your conversation. I have known you from your youth since we have dwelt in one parish together. There, as you yourself can tell (I am sorry you compel me to say so), you were esteemed to be very light of tongue, a great dicer, and of no commendable fame.

Thomas then appealed directly to the judges and members of the jury, especially to those like Cromwell and Audley who had interrogated him earlier:

Can it therefore seem likely to your honorable lordships that I would, in so weighty matter a cause, so unadvisedly overshoot myself as to trust Master Rich, a man by me always reputed for one of very little truth, as your lordships have heard…, that I would utter to him the secrets of my conscience touching the king's supremacy… a thing I never did, nor never would, after the statute was made, reveal to the king's highness himself, or to any of his honorable councilors, as it is not unknown to your honors, at sundry several times sent from his grace's own person to the Tower to me for no other purpose? Can this in your judgments, my lords, seem likely to be true?

Having demolished Rich's credibility, Thomas then turned to the charge that he had spoken maliciously. Even if he and Rich had discussed hypothetical cases in a private conversation, he said, "it cannot justly be taken to be spoken maliciously, and where there is no malice, there can be no offense." He explained that "malice" had a precise meaning in the law and in this case it was equivalent to the term "forcible."

Thomas then proceeded to establish his own credibility, reviewing his service to the king over a period of twenty years.

During all that time, no fault had ever been found and the king had publicly expressed his appreciation. How could the word of a man like Rich stand up against his?

Rich then asked that Richard Southwell and Thomas Palmer be called as witnesses since they were with him at the time of the conversation. Both men testified that they were too busy confiscating Thomas's books and writing materials to pay attention to the conversation.

At that the jury was asked to give a verdict. After deliberating all of fifteen minutes, it returned the verdict of guilty. But Thomas wasn't finished. He had one more legal maneuver he could try. As Audley was about to pass sentence on him, Thomas interrupted: "My lord, when I was toward the law, the manner in such case was to ask the prisoner before judgment, why judgment should not be given against him."

Audley was clearly discomfited, but asked, "What, then are you able to say to the contrary?"

Thomas then challenged the legitimacy of the law under which he was being condemned. He said:

> Inasmuch, my lord, as this indictment is grounded upon an Act of Parliament directly repugnant to the laws of God and his holy Church, the supreme government of which, or of any part thereof, may no temporal prince presume by any law to take upon him as rightfully belonging to the See of Rome, a spiritual preeminence by the mouth of Our Savior himself, personally present upon the earth, only to Saint Peter and his successors, bishops of the same See, by special prerogative guaranteed, it is therefore in law among Christian men insufficient to charge any Christian man.
>
> This realm, being but one member and small part of the Church, might not make a particular law disagreeable with the general law of Christ's universal

Catholic Church any more than the city of London, being but one poor member in respect of the whole realm, might make a law against an Act of Parliament to bind the whole realm. No more might this realm of England refuse obedience to the See of Rome than might a child refuse obedience to his own natural father.

Thomas gave examples that showed that the provisions of the Act of Succession and the Act of Treasons violated many other laws that had never been repealed, including the Magna Carta, the first clause of which guaranteed that "the English Church shall be free, and shall have its rights undiminished and its liberties unimpaired." He also quoted scriptural texts to prove that no layman could be head of the Church.

Audley interrupted to ask how Thomas could presume to challenge the bishops, universities and the "best learned of this realm." Thomas replied:

If the number of bishops and universities should be so material as your lordship seems to think, then I see little cause, my lord, why that should make any change in my conscience. For I have no doubt that, though not in this realm, but of all those well learned bishops and virtuous men that are yet alive through-out Christendom, they are not fewer who are of my mind. But if I should speak of those who are already dead, of whom many are now holy saints in heaven, I am very sure it is the far greater part of them who, all the while they lived, thought in this case the way that I think now. And therefore I am not bound, my lord, to conform my conscience to the council of one realm against the General Council of Christendom.

This argument appeared to hit home. Audley was clearly uncomfortable. Finally he turned to Lord Fitz-James, chief justice of the King's Bench, and asked his opinion. There was a long silence before Fitz-James finally gave this confusing and ambiguous reply: "I must confess that if the act of Parliament is not unlawful, then is not the indictment in my conscience insufficient."

Whether or not Audley understood what Fitz-James was trying to say, he turned to Thomas and said, "You are judged to be guilty, Sir Thomas More. Do you have anything else to allege for your defense? We will grant you favorable audience."

Thomas replied:

> More have I not to say, my lords, but that like the blessed apostle Saint Paul, as we read in the Acts of the Apostles, was present, and consented to the death of Saint Stephen, and kept their clothes that stoned him to death, and yet they now are both holy saints in heaven, and shall continue there friends forever, so I trust, and shall therefore heartily pray, that though your lordships have now here on earth been judges to my condemnation, we may yet hereafter in heaven merrily all meet together, to our everlasting salvation and thus I desire Almighty God to preserve and defend the king's majesty, and to send him good counsel.

Audley then pronounced sentence: "Sir Thomas More, you are to be drawn on a hurdle through the City of London to Tyburn, there to be hanged till you be half dead, after that cut down yet alive, your bowels to be taken out of your body and burned before you, your private parts cut off, your head cut off, your body to be divided in four parts, and your head and body to be set at such places as the king shall assign."

His Final Days and His Execution

Thomas was then taken back to the Tower. Meg and William Roper were waiting for him and Meg, after first kneeling in the street to get Thomas's blessing, threw her arms about him and kissed him. They talked briefly and Meg began to walk away, but then turned back and ran to him again, and, as Roper wrote later, "took him about the neck, and divers times together most lovingly kissed him." Roper also reported that many in the large crowd that had gathered to see the famous prisoner were mourning and weeping.

During the last five days of his life, Thomas fasted and prayed. He had no paper and ink, but was allowed a slate on which he could write. It apparently was brought to him by Dorothy Colley, Meg's servant, who had been given permission to visit him each day. He composed a final prayer, copied by Meg sometime later. In it he lamented his sinful life and expressed his hope to be with God, "not for the avoiding of the calamities of this wretched world" but "for a very love of thee."

Alice was permitted a final visit with her husband the day before his execution. We don't know what transpired between them except that Thomas gave Alice his hair shirt and a letter to Meg that he had written with a piece of coal. In it he expressed his wish to die the next day, the feast of the translation of the relics of Saint Thomas Becket. He also told her, "I never liked your manner better than when you kissed me last. For I like when daughterly love and dear charity has no leisure to look to worldly courtesy." He blessed his family and asked them to pray for him.

We don't know when Thomas learned that King Henry had commuted the sentence passed on him by Thomas Audley, from hanging and disembowelment to beheading. The king said that he granted this favor because of Thomas's long service.

On July 6, 1535, Thomas Pope, a representative of the king's council, advised Thomas that he was to die at nine o'clock that morning. He also told him that the king wished him not to "use many words" before the execution. Thomas thanked Pope for the warning and said that he would conform to the king's command, although he was certain that the king would not be offended by what he had planned to say.

His family was not permitted to witness the execution, but a large crowd gathered as he was led to the scaffold, and his various biographers reported some of the shouts directed his way. A woman called out that Thomas had kept some evidence that belonged to her when she appeared before him at a trial, and asked that he now request that she might have it. Thomas replied, "Good woman, have patience a little while, for the king is good to me that even within this half-hour he will discharge me of all business, and will help you himself."

Another woman called out that he had not been just to her during her trial. Thomas answered, "Woman, I remember well the whole matter. If now I were to give sentence again, I assure you, I would not alter it."

Someone offered him a cup of wine, which he declined, saying, "My master had vinegar and gall, not wine, given him to drink."

He needed assistance climbing the steps to the scaffold and asked one of the sheriffs to give him a hand. He said, "When I come down again, let me shift for myself as well as I can."

As the king had asked, he spoke only briefly to the crowd, asking them to pray for him in this world and he would pray for them in the next. He also told them to pray for the king that he might receive good counsel. He said, "I die the king's good servant but God's first."

He knelt and recited Psalm 51, known as the *Miserere*. He rose and, according to custom, the executioner knelt before him and begged his forgiveness and blessing. Thomas said, "You will give me this day a greater benefit than ever any mortal man can be able to give me. Pluck up your spirits, man, and don't be afraid to do your office. My neck is very short, so take heed you don't strike awry for saving your honesty."

He knelt and put his head across the block. But then he signaled for the executioner to wait. He carefully stretched out his long beard saying, "I pray you let me lay my beard over the block lest you should cut it. At least that has committed no treason."

He was killed with one stroke of the axe. His body was taken to the Church of St. Peter ad Vincula (in Chains) within the Tower where it was interred. His head was boiled, impaled on a pole and displayed on London Bridge. Later it was buried in the Roper Vault at St. Dunstan's Church in Canterbury.

EPILOGUE

In dying when he did, Thomas More escaped the worst of the persecution of the Catholic Church in England. His execution and that of John Fisher ushered in a particularly bloody period in English history.

Only from heaven did Thomas know what would happen to Henry VIII. Ten months after Thomas's execution, Henry also had Queen Anne (Boleyn) beheaded, charging her with adultery after she bore him a daughter, Elizabeth, instead of the son he wanted. He married Jane Seymour, who died after giving birth to their son, Edward. Henry then married Anne of Cleves, a marriage arranged by Thomas Cromwell for diplomatic purposes, but Henry grew tired of her; he divorced her and had Cromwell executed. His fifth wife, Catherine Howard, was beheaded in 1542 and his sixth wife, Catherine Parr, was about to be executed when Henry died in 1547.

Meanwhile, as Thomas probably expected, Henry launched a great raid on ecclesiastical property, suppressing the monasteries and taking their assets, which he distributed to the nobility. Despite this, Henry always considered himself an orthodox Catholic. In fact, he enacted the Six Articles in 1539, reaffirming traditional Catholic doctrine including transubstantiation, the sufficiency of Communion under one species, priestly celibacy, the validity of the vow of chastity, Masses for the souls in purgatory, and auricular confession.

Henry was survived by three legitimate children—Mary, daughter of Catherine of Aragon; Elizabeth, daughter of Anne Boleyn; and Edward, son of Jane Seymour. Edward, the only male, became king at age ten, reigning as Edward VI. He was reared as a Protestant. The "Book of Common Prayer" was issued in 1549 and this is considered the first official act of England's conversion to Protestantism. The book substituted a Communion Service in English for the Mass in Latin and sanctioned Protestant views of the Eucharist.

Edward was king for only six years before he died in 1553. He was succeeded by Mary, the daughter of Henry VIII and Catherine of Aragon. A devout Catholic like her mother, she has gone down in history as "Bloody Mary" because, in her zeal to return the country to Catholicism, she sent about two hundred seventy-five persons to death by burning, including Thomas Cranmer, Archbishop of Canterbury.

Mary, though, was queen for only five years. She was succeeded by her half-sister Elizabeth, daughter of Henry VIII and Anne Boleyn. She returned the country to Protestantism. In 1563 Parliament promulgated thirty-nine articles that repudiated many Catholic doctrines. During the following twenty years, two hundred twenty-one Catholics were put to death. Elizabeth reigned for forty-five years, until her death in 1603.

Persecution of the Catholic Church in England continued through the seventeenth century. By the time King William's reign ended in 1702, Catholics had dwindled to less than one percent of the population in a country that had been thoroughly Catholic. They couldn't even acquire, own and inherit property until 1778. Further concessions were made by the Catholic Relief Act in 1791. In 1829 the Catholic Emancipation Act relieved Catholics of both England and Ireland of most of the civil disabilities to which they had been subject. In 1850 the Church had its hierarchy restored. Finally, in 1926 another Catholic Relief Act repealed virtually all legal disabilities of Catholics in England.

The nineteenth and twentieth centuries saw a number of converts from the Anglican Church to Catholicism, the most notable of which were Cardinal John Henry Newman and Gilbert Keith Chesterton. Today the number of Catholics in England continues to grow, not only through converts but also from immigration, especially immigrants from Poland. Meanwhile, the Anglican Church is losing members as only a small minority of the British people goes to church.

THOMAS'S GROWING REPUTATION AFTER HIS DEATH

As for Thomas More, his reputation grew after his death even more than during his lifetime, even though he was famous throughout Europe while he lived. William Roper wrote the first biography of his father-in-law, but others soon followed. Perhaps the most surprising writing is the play *Sir Thomas More*, written by several playwrights including William Shakespeare, that was written late in the sixteenth century while Queen Elizabeth I, Henry VIII's daughter, was still reigning.

In 1929 the English writer Hilaire Belloc noted that the sacrifice that Thomas made of his life had become larger and larger in people's eyes with every passing decade and, "I can believe that a hundred years hence he will appear as one of the ten chief men of that great time. He already appears among the first hundred."

Other famous writers (including G.K. Chesterton, whose quote begins the Foreword to this book) also praised Thomas. John Donne said that he was "a man of the most tender and delicate conscience that the world saw since Augustine." And Jonathan Swift, the Anglican clergyman known mainly as author of *Gulliver's Travels*, went so far as to call him "a person of the greatest virtue this kingdom ever produced."

In 1969 a larger-than-life bronze statue of Thomas was unveiled in Chelsea, London, by the Speaker of the House of Commons. Among those at the unveiling were the Archbishop of Canterbury and the Archbishop of Westminster.

As for the Catholic Church, it seemed to have forgotten Thomas for several centuries since he wasn't beatified until Pope Leo XIII did it in 1886. This is because the Church didn't want to antagonize a hostile government in England, hoping that conditions for Catholics there would improve. After the Church's hierarchy was restored in 1850, the newly appointed archbishop began the lengthy process that finally led to beatification and canonization.

THE OBJECT OF OUR IMITATION

Pope Pius XI canonized both Thomas More and John Fisher on May 19, 1935, four hundred years after their deaths. At the time Adolf Hitler had gained control of Germany and the pope presented Thomas as a model for German Catholics. He said that Thomas was a "strong and courageous spirit" who "knew how to despise resolutely the flattery of human respect, how to resist, in accordance with his duty, the supreme head of the state."

He then said the words that are the theme of this book:

The two great figures which today are upraised before us as objects of our admiration ought also to be the object of our imitation; and, although they are two such grand personalities, yet such imitation is not difficult, but possible.

There are, in fact, many opportunities for imitating the martyrs without the martyrdom of blood and death. There is a martyrdom which consists in the anguish which each of us experiences in himself in following the ways of God and in the fulfillment of his proper duty. There is a martyrdom which consists in the difficulty of a duty exactly, faithfully, and fully accomplished. There is a martyrdom which occurs in the continual persevering fidelity in little things, in those demands for diligence in the divine service, in the daily duty which becomes a daily cross.

In September of 2004, Bishop Michael A. Saltarelli of Wilmington, Delaware, issued the following prayer "for politicians who take public anti-life positions":

(Repeat after each invocation "Pray for us.")

St. Thomas More, Saint and Martyr

St. Thomas More, Patron of Statesmen, Politicians and Lawyers

St. Thomas More, Patron of Justices, Judges and Magistrates

St. Thomas More, Model of Integrity and Virtue in Public and Private Life

St. Thomas More, Servant of the Word of God and the Body and Blood of Christ

St. Thomas More, Model of Holiness in the Sacrament of Marriage

St. Thomas More, Teacher of His Children in the Catholic Faith

St. Thomas More, Defender of the Weak and the Poor

St. Thomas More, Promoter of Human Life and Dignity

Let us pray: Oh glorious St. Thomas More, patron of statesmen, politicians, judges, and lawyers, your life of prayer and penance, and your zeal for justice, integrity and firm principle in public and family life led you to the path of martyrdom and sainthood. Intercede for our statesmen, politicians, judges and lawyers, that they may be courageous and effective in their defense and promotion of the sanctity of human life—the foundation of all other human rights. We ask this through Christ Our Lord. Amen.

St. Thomas More can be a model not only for all those mentioned in Bishop Saltarelli's prayer, but for all Catholics.

ACKNOWLEDGMENTS

There have been so many books written about Saint Thomas More, or books written by him, that the bibliography of Peter Ackroyd's scholarly book *The Life of Thomas More* takes thirteen pages. I'm not going to include nearly that many.

In acknowledging my sources for this book, I should start with Thomas's own writings, and two American universities have made that easy for us. Beginning in 1963 and ending in 1987, Yale University published *The Complete Works of St. Thomas More* in fifteen volumes. Prior to that, in 1947, Princeton University published *The Correspondence of Sir Thomas More*. These have proved invaluable for biographers ever since.

I first discovered Yale's fifteen volumes in 1997 in the library of the Tantur Institute for Ecumenical Studies in Jerusalem, where I studied for three months. I had just retired as editor of *The Criterion*, newspaper of the Archdiocese of Indianapolis, and was preparing myself to write Catholic books in my retirement. One of the books I had in mind was *Married Saints*, which would, of course, include a chapter about St. Thomas More. I can't claim to have read all fifteen volumes, but I sampled writings from most of them, including, of course, *Utopia* and several of Thomas's books in defense of the Church. I read enough in *Confutation of Tyndale's Answer* to agree with Thomas's own criticism that his writing was overlong and too tedious.

As for books about Saint Thomas More, I began with William Roper's biography. Several publishers have published editions of this book, but the one I used was published by J.M.

Dent & Sons Ltd. in London and E.P. Dutton & Co., Inc., New York, in 1906. I then went to the entry on Thomas in *Our Sunday Visitor's Encyclopedia of Saints* as a check to make sure I covered the most important aspects of Thomas's life.

I mentioned above the biography written by Peter Ackroyd. This 447-page scholarly work was published by Doubleday in 1998 and is, therefore, one of the more recent books about Thomas. It undoubtedly was my most important source for this book.

An even more recent book is *In the Lion's Court: Power, Ambition, and Sudden Death in the Reign of Henry VIII*, by Derek Wilson, published by St. Martin's Press in 2001. It, too, is a scholarly treatment, not only of Thomas More, but also of five other Thomases—Wolsey, Cromwell, Howard, Cranmer, and Wriothesley (who isn't mentioned in my book). I should note that this book is not as kind to Thomas as are most of his biographers.

Another important source was *Thomas More: A Portrait of Courage*, by Gerard B. Wegemer, published in 1995 by Scepter Publishers, Inc. Still another was *Born for Friendship: The Spirit of Sir Thomas More*, by Rev. Bernard Basset, S.J., published by Sheed and Ward in 1965. Finally there was *Thomas More*, by Anne Murphy, published by Triumph in 1996 as part of its "Great Christian Thinkers" series.

These, then, served as my major sources for this book, although I also dipped into a few other books included in the Bibliography.

SELECTED BIBLIOGRAPHY

Ackroyd, Peter. *The Life of Thomas More* (1998).

Augustine, Saint. *City of God*, H. Bettenson trans. (1972).

Basset, Bernard. *Born for Friendship* (1965).

Beck, W. *Sir Thomas More* (1862).

Belloc, Hilaire. *How the Reformation Happened* (1928).

Bolt, Robert. *A Man for All Seasons* (play & movie) (1966).

Bourne-Jones, D. *Merrily to Meet: A Poetic Study of Sir Thomas More* (1987).

Boutrais, C. *The Monastery of the Great Chartreuse* (1983).

Bridgett, T.E. *Life and Writings of Sir Thomas More* (1891).

Bunsun, Matthew, Margaret, Stephen. *Our Sunday Visitor's Encyclopedia of Saints* (1998).

Byron, B. *Loyalty in the Spirituality of Saint Thomas More* (1971).

Campbell, W.E. *Erasmus, Tyndale and More* (1949).

Cecil, A. *A Portrait of Thomas More: Scholar, Statesman, Saint* (1937).

Chambers, R.W. *The Place of Saint Thomas More in English Literature and History* (1937).

_____ *The Saga and the Myth of Sir Thomas More* (1927).

_____ *Thomas More* (1935).

Charlton, K. *Education in Renaissance England* (1965).

Clark, F.L. *William Warham: Archbishop of Canterbury, 1504-1532* (1993).

Davies, R. *Chelsea Old Church* (1904).

Doernberg, E. *Henry VIII and Luther* (1961).

Elton, G.R. *England under the Tudors* (1955).

_____ *Reform and Reformation: England 1509-1558* (1977).

Erasmus, Desiderius. *Pilgrimages* (1849).

_____ *Letters*, F.M. Nichols trans. and ed., 3 vols. (1901-18).

_____ *Praise of Folly*, John Wilson trans. (1668).

_____ *Colloquies*, Roger L'Estrange trans. (1923).

_____ *The Education of a Christian Prince*, Lester K. Born trans. (1936).

Farrow, J. *The Story of Thomas More* (1956).

Fink, John F. *Married Saints* (1992).

_____ *Moments in Catholic History* (1992).

Flower, B.O. *The Century of Sir Thomas More* (1896).

Fox, A. *Thomas More: History and Providence* (1982).

_____ *Politics and Literature in the Reigns of Henry VII & Henry VIII* (1989).

Fox, A. and J. Guy. *Reassessing the Henrician Age* (1986).

Gairdner, J. *Letters and Papers of the Reign of Henry VIII*, vols. 1-5 (1880).

Gleason, John B. *John Colet* (1989).

Gogan, Brian. *The Common Corps of Christendom: Ecclesiological Themes in the Writings of Sir Thomas More* (1962).

Guy, John A. *The Cardinal's Court: The Impact of Thomas Wolsey in the Star Chamber* (1977).

_____ *The Public Career of Sir Thomas More* (1980).

_____ *Tudor England* (1988).

Gwyn, Peter. *The King's Cardinal: The Rise and Fall of Thomas Wolsey* (1990).

Haigh, Christopher. *English Reformations: Religion, Politics and Society under the Tudors* (1993).

Halkin, L.C. *Erasmus* (1987).

Hanham, A. *Richard III and His Early Historians, 1482-1535* (1975).

Harpsfield, N. *The Life and Death of Thomas More* (1932).

Haughton, R. *The Young Thomas More* (1966).

Hendricks, L. *The London Charterhouse* (1889).

Hilderbrand, H.J. *Erasmus and His Age* (1970).

Hill, D. *Hans Holbein* (1959).

Hogrefe, P. *The Sir Thomas More Circle* (1959).

Hollis, Christopher. *Sir Thomas More* (1936).

Hope, W.H. Saint-John. *The History of the London Charterhouse from its Foundation until the Suppression of the Monastery* (1925).

Hurst, G. *A Short History of Lincoln's Inn* (1946).

Hutton, W.H. *Sir Thomas More* (1900).

Kautsky, Karl. *Thomas More and His Utopia* (1927).

Kenny, Anthony. *Thomas More* (1983).

Kinney, A.F. *Rhetoric and Poetic in Thomas More's Utopia* (1979).

Knowles, D. and W.F. Grimes. *Charterhouse* (1954).

Knox, D.B. *The Doctrine of the Faith in the Reign of Henry VIII* (1961).

Langdon, H. *Holbein* (1976).

Lee, S. *Great Englishmen of the Sixteenth Century* (1904).

Lehmberg, S.E. *The Reformation Parliament* (1970).

Lewis, C.S. *English Literature in the Sixteenth Century Excluding Drama* (1954).

Loades, David. *The Tudor Court* (1986).

Logan, G.M. *The Meaning of More's 'Utopia'* (1983).

MacCulloch, Diarmaid. *Thomas Cranmer* (1996).

Manning, A. *The Household of Sir Thomas More* (1851).

Marius, Richard. *Thomas More* (1984).

Martz, Louis L. *Thomas More: The Search for the Inner Man* (1990).

Martz, Louis and R.S. Sylvester. (eds.), *Thomas More's Prayer Book* (1969).

Mason, A.J. *Lectures on Colet, Fisher & More* (1895).

Matthew, Sister M. *Saint Thomas More* (1951).

Maynard, T. *Humanist and Hero: Life of Sir Thomas More* (1947).

Moore, M.J. (ed.), *Quincentennial Essays on Saint Thomas More* (1978).

Moorman, J.R.H. *A History of the Church in England* (1953).

More, Cresacre. *The Life and Death of Sir Thomas More* (1631).

More, Thomas. *The Correspondence of Sir Thomas More*, E.F. Rogers, ed. (1947).

_____ *The Yale Edition of the Complete Works of St. Thomas More*, various editors (1963-1987).

Morison, S. *The Likeness of Thomas More* (1963).

Murphy, Anne. *Thomas More* (1996).

Neame, Alan. *The Holy Maid of Kent* (1971).

Norrington, Ruth. *In the Shadow of a Saint: Lady Alice More* (1983).

Olin, J.C. (ed.), *Interpreting Thomas More's Utopia* (1989).

Orme, Nicholas. *English Schools in the Middle Ages* (1973).

Paul, J.E. *Catherine of Aragon and Her Friends* (1966).

Paul, L.A. *Sir Thomas More* (1953).

Pickthorn, K. *Early Tudor Government*, 2 vols. (1934).

Pineas, R. *Thomas More and Tudor Polemics* (1968).

Pollard, A.F. *Wolsey* (1965).

Reynolds, E.E. *Saint John Fisher* (1965).

_____ *The Trial of Saint Thomas More* (1964).

_____ *Sir Thomas More* (1965).

_____ *Thomas More and Erasmus* (1965).

_____ *The Field Is Won: The Life and Death of St. Thomas More* (1968).

Rope, H.E.G. *Fisher and More* (1935).

Roper, William. *The Life of Sir Thomas More* (Dutton, 1906).

_____ *The Life of Sir Thomas More*, S.W. Singer, ed. (1822).

_____ *The Lyfe of Sir Thomas Moore, Knight*, Elsie V. Hitchcock, ed. (1935).

Routh, E.M.G. *Sir Thomas More and His Friends* (1934).

Rupp, G. *Thomas More* (1978).

Sargeant, Daniel. *Thomas More* (1934).

Scarisbrick, J.J. *Henry VIII* (1976).

Shebbeare, C.E. *Sir Thomas More* (1930).

Slavin, A.J. (ed.), *Humanism, Reform and the Reformation in England* (1969).

Smith, R.L. *John Fisher and Thomas More: Two English Saints* (1935).

Somerville, R. *The Duchy of Lancaster* (1946).

Stapleton, Thomas. *Life of Sir Thomas More*, E.E. Reynolds, ed. (1966).

Starkey, David. *The Reign of Henry VIII* (1985).

Stewart, Agnes M. *Margaret Roper or the Chancellor and His Daughter* (1875).

_____ *The Life and Letters of Sir Thomas More* (1876).

Stobbart, Lorraine. *Utopia: Fact or Fiction?* (1992).

Sturge, C. *Cuthbert Tunstall* (1938).

Surtz, Edward L. *The Works and Days of John Fisher* (1967).

Swanson, R.N. *Church and Society in Late Medieval England* (1989).

Sylvester, R.S. (ed.). *Saint Thomas More: Action and Contemplation* (1972).

Teetgen, A.B. *The Footsteps of Thomas More* (1930).

Thigpen, Paul (compiler). *Be Merry in God* (Reflections from the writings of Thomas More) (1999).

Thomas More College. *Thomas More Quincentennial Conference* (1978).

Thompson, Craig R. *The Translation of Lucian by Erasmus and Saint Thomas More* (1940).

Thompson, E.M. *The Carthusian Order in England* (1930).

Thurston, H. and D. Attwater. *Butler's Lives of the Saints* (1956).

Tracy, J.D. *Erasmus: The Growth of a Mind* (1972).

Trapp, J.B. *Erasmus, Colet and More: The Early Tudor Humanists and their Books* (1991).

Trapp, J.B. and H.S. Herbruggen. *'The King's Good Servant'* (1977).

Walker, J.W. *Sir Thomas More: His Life and Times* (1840).

Wegemer, Gerard B. *Thomas More: A Portrait of Courage* (1995).

Williams, C.H. *England under the Tudors* (1925).

Willow, M.E. *The English Poems of Saint Thomas More* (1974).

Wilson, Derek. *England in the Age of Thomas More* (1978).

_____ *In the Lion's Court* (2001).

Woodhouse, R.I. *The Life of Archbishop Morton* (1895).

Wrench, M. *The Story of Thomas More* (1961).